THE LONDON TO BRIGHTON LINE

THROUGH TIME

Simon Jeffs

AMBERLEY PUBLISHING

First published 2013

Amberley Publishing
The Hill, Stroud
Gloucestershire, GL5 4EP

www.amberley-books.com

Copyright © Simon Jeffs , 2013

The right of Simon Jeffs
to be identified as the Author of this work
has been asserted in accordance with the
Copyrights, Designs and Patents Act 1988.

ISBN 978 1 4456 0979 9

British Library Cataloguing in Publication Data.
A catalogue record for this book is available from
the British Library.

Typeset in 9.5pt on 12pt Celeste.
Typesetting by Amberley Publishing.
Printed in the UK.

A Brief History of the 'Brighton'

The history of the London–Brighton line starts with John Rennie's proposal to connect the Metropolis with Brighton receiving Royal Assent on 15 July 1837, authorizing the London & Brighton Railway (LBR) to build a line from a junction with the London & Croydon Railway (LCR) near Croydon to Brighton, with branches to Shoreham and Newhaven. Construction work started in March 1838, with David Mocatta appointed as architect and John Rastrick as the resident Engineer.

An important aspect of the LBR Act was the Government's insistence that the LBR and South Eastern Railway (SER) must share a route into London. The SER was thus forced to deviate via Red Hill (sic), where their line to Dover branched off. From Jolly Sailor (Norwood Junction) to Corbetts Lane Junction in South London, both companies would use the tracks of the LCR, which had opened its line from West Croydon to Corbetts Lane Junction on 5 June 1839, with intermediate stations at Jolly Sailor (Norwood Junction), Annerley (now Anerley), Penge (now Penge West), Sydenham, Dartmouth Arms (now Forest Hill) and New Cross (now New Cross Gate); then all three companies would use the tracks of the London & Greenwich Railway (LGR – opened from Deptford on 14 December 1836) to London Bridge. Work on the coastal branch proceeded rapidly and the ceremonial opening of the Brighton–Shoreham branch took place on 11 May 1840, while work on the main line was advanced enough for services to operate between Haywards Heath and London Bridge from 12 July 1841. Intermediate stations were provided at Croydon (later East Croydon), Godstone Road (later Purley), Stoats Nest, Merstham, Red-Hill and Reigate Road, Horley, Three Bridges and Balcombe, and later at Burgess Hill and Hassocks. Finally, the great day dawned on 21 September 1841, when the directors of the line and other dignitaries were conveyed in two trains from London Bridge to Brighton. The Metropolis and Brighton were now connected, but Brighton tried to ensure that its high-class clientele would not be frightened away by hordes of unwashed 'excursionists'. Hence, its first timetable of seven trains a day included three for First Class passengers only!

The LBR soon ran up against economic reality. Receipts were poor, not least due to the lack of Third Class passengers and excursionists, while the upper classes deserted Brighton for the Continental resorts. The town was forced to accept the excursionists or decay and so, on Easter Monday 1844, the first train steamed into Brighton from London conveying the lower orders for a day at the seaside. Day Trips to Brighton had started – and have continued ever since. The SER and LGR amalgamated in 1845, while the LBR absorbed the LCR to become the London, Brighton & South Coast Railway (LBSCR) in July 1846. This certainly eased the situation at London Bridge, but periodic spats continued between the LBSCR and SER for many years, particularly over Redhill.

A key feature in the further development of Brighton Line services was the Great Exhibition, held in Hyde Park in 1851. Two of the LBSCR directors were instrumental in re-erecting the glass exhibition hall, known as the Crystal Palace, in Penge Park, believing that this would bring much extra traffic to the LBSCR. A short branch running from south of Sydenham to the Crystal Palace terminal was available to passengers from June 1854, when the Palace was officially opened by Queen Victoria. This was extended to the Thames at Battersea in March 1858, where the station was named Pimlico, doubtless to enhance the location's social cachet! Two years later, the Thames was bridged and Victoria station was opened to passengers on 1 October 1860 and the direct line from Croydon to Balham (where it joined the Crystal Palace line) opened in December 1862. To complete the Victoria story, the high-level approach from near Clapham Junction to Battersea Park was opened in December 1867 and is the one used by all Brighton line services today. Now Brighton was as close to Victoria in travelling time to London Bridge, and the LBSCR had both City and West End termini.

Other lines soon joined the LBSCR system in London: the South London Line from Victoria, famed as one of the pioneers of electric traction from 1909, joined the London Bridge line in August 1866; the East London Line reached the New Cross stations of the SER and LBSCR in December 1869, eventually becoming part of the Underground system on electrification in March 1913; meanwhile, over in West London, the creation of Clapham Junction in March 1863 was due to the arrival of the West London Extension Railway (WLER), which linked the London & North Western Railway (LNWR) and the Great Western Railway (GWR) through Kensington to the lines south of the Thames.

From the 1860s, the Brighton system expanded. The main line between both London termini and Balcombe Tunnel Junction (south of Three Bridges) was progressively quadrupled between 1864 and 1910. Indeed, plans were obtained to continue the four-track railway all the way to Brighton, but the sheer cost of extra tunnels and viaducts was prohibitive and line capacity has suffered ever since. New stations were opened at Brockley, Norbury, Honor Oak Park, Coulsdon South, Purley Oaks and Stoats Nest (later Coulsdon North) during this period. The Cliftonville Curve, allowing through running between Preston Park, Hove and the West Coastway line, was opened in July 1879 and Brighton station extensively rebuilt in 1883 to cope with the town's growing population. By the end of the nineteenth century, Redhill was becoming congested, and a new railway was built between Coulsdon and Earlswood to bypass the junction. Heavy engineering works were required to get the line through the Downs, involving two tunnels and deep cuttings through the chalk and sand. The Quarry Line, as it became known, opened on 1 April 1900.

Thus, by 1910, the infrastructure of Brighton Main Line was recognizably the railway we know today. The next leap forward was technological.

In 1901/2 a number of schemes for new electric lines, or even monorails, between London and Brighton, had come to fruition. The LBSCR responded by publicising its Earlswood–Preston Park quadrupling project and stating that they would then have two tracks for the latest novelties in traction, '... whether in the direction of electric cars or navigable balloons'. It also showed that steam traction could be pretty quick as well. A demonstration run with a B4 class loco sprinted from London Bridge to Brighton in 48 minutes 41 seconds in July 1903. But the Brighton was not averse to electrification and was a pioneer in its widespread adoption of electric traction. Powers were obtained in July 1903 to electrify all of its lines, with an initial emphasis on the Company's suburban network but with an eye firmly on extension to Brighton. Using a 6,700 V 25 Hz AC overhead power supply system, the first line to be electrified was the South London Line between Victoria and London Bridge. Public services commenced on the 'Elevated Electric' on 1 December 1909 and were followed by extensions to Crystal Palace (in 1911) and Coulsdon North (in 1925, by the Southern Railway).

The LBSCR now entered a Golden Age and the summer timetable of 1912 showed an unprecedented thirty-three through trains between London and Brighton. However, storm clouds were gathering over Europe and the First World War had a considerable effect on Brighton line services, the saddest legacy being the number of LBSCR employees who lost their lives in the conflict and are commemorated in the memorial at Victoria station. The last steam loco built by the LBSCR, a massive Billinton 4-6-4 tank engine which left Brighton Works in 1922, was named *Remembrance* as a moving tribute to the 532 men who lost their lives.

On 1 January 1923, the Southern Railway (SR) came into being, combining the LBSCR, South Eastern & Chatham Railway (SECR), LSWR and a number of other minor companies. The SR appointed Sir Herbert Walker as its General Manager and on 10 October 1929, he presented his plans to electrify from Coulsdon North to Brighton and Worthing using the now familiar third rail 660 V DC system. Public services to Brighton commenced on 1 January 1933, providing unprecedented frequencies between Brighton, Worthing and the Metropolis. New electric multiple units (EMUs) were built for express, Pullman, semi-fast and slow services. Further extensions of the third rail to Eastbourne and Ore followed in July 1935, and between Dorking and Ford, Three Bridges to Horsham and West Worthing to Havant (including the Bognor Regis and Littlehampton branches) by July 1938, relegating steam traction on the Brighton Line to goods, excursion traffic, the Newhaven Boat Trains, services to Horsham via Steyning, to East Grinstead, to Tonbridge and regular services to Plymouth, the GWR and the LMSR. A new station was opened at Tinsley Green on 13 November 1935 to serve the embryonic Gatwick Airport, from where commercial flights commenced the following May.

Unlike the First World War, the Brighton Line was very much on the front line during the Second World War. Mass evacuations of children from South London occurred in September 1939; services were cut by half, with Eastbourne and Worthing passengers often having to change at Brighton; and nearly all holiday trains from north of the Thames were curtailed. Most buffet and restaurant cars were withdrawn and the Brighton Belle EMUs were stored from May 1942. Brighton Works were re-equipped in 1942 and started making locomotives again. Later, the Blitz caused severe damage to London Bridge, Victoria and Brighton. Redhill was at the forefront of the Dunkirk evacuation, with evacuees from Kent passing through. Engines were changed in 4 minutes or even less and over 300 tons of ash accumulated in the shed yard. If ever a Brighton station deserved a medal, it was Redhill.

After the war, the railways were left in a very run-down condition and were Nationalised from 1 January 1948. The Brighton line became the Central Division of the Southern Region of British Railways (BR). The 1954 Modernisation Plan and 1963 Beeching Report led to the final withdrawal of steam from the line by 1965 (and the closure of Brighton Works) and their replacement by diesel, electric and electro-diesel locomotives and diesel electric multiple units (DEMUs); a fleet of new EMUs (the Cig/Big/Vep stock) to replace the Maunsell-era stock; the closure of virtually all small and many larger goods yards by 1970; and the withdrawal of passenger and freight services on many secondary lines, particularly in the High Weald of Sussex. On 27 May 1958, the Racecourse station at Gatwick Airport was closed and a replacement opened to serve the new, enlarged Gatwick Airport. Thus began the relentless growth of Gatwick and the train services that came to serve it.

Throughout the 1950s, 1960s and 1970s, passenger traffic on the Brighton Line increased, aided by the expansion of Croydon as a business and commercial centre; the development of Crawley new town; the opening of Brighton University and the general expansion of secondary and tertiary education; and the centralisation of job markets in London, and to a lesser extent at Croydon, Brighton and Gatwick.

In 1982, the BR regions were abolished and British Rail was split into business sectors, the Southern Region becoming part of the London & South Eastern (L&SE) sector, stretching from Exeter in the west to Kings Lynn in the east. In 1986, L&SE was re-launched as Network SouthEast (NSE) and extensively developed. Two outcomes of sectorisation had major impacts on the Brighton line. First, Thameslink, a project that connected the northern and southern halves of London's suburban network via the re-opened Snow Hill tunnel between Blackfriars and Farringdon in 1988, bringing through services between Brighton, Blackfriars, Luton and Bedford and a fleet of new trains to operate them. Second, the InterCity sector took over the Gatwick Airport–Victoria rail link, rebranded it as Gatwick Express and operated a non-stopservice every fifteen minutes using air-conditioned coaches from May 1984.These trains ran on a newly resignalled line after the London Bridge (completed 1975), Victoria and Three Bridges (both completed 1983) projects. Associated with these schemes were the remodelling of London Bridge between 1972–8 and the complex of junctions north of East Croydon (1983), the closure and subsequent demolition of Coulsdon North and the replacement of all signal boxes along the Brighton main line by three signalling centres at London Bridge, Clapham Junction and Three Bridges.

The railways were privatised from 1 April 1994, with track and associated signaling (plus Victoria, London Bridge and Gatwick Airport stations) being transferred to a not-for-profit Government-owned 'company', Railtrack (later Network Rail), while passenger and goods services were let as franchises by the Government, to be operated by train-operating companies (TOCs). The situation on the Brighton Line was particularly complex, as passenger service groups were parcelled up into the Gatwick Express, South Central, Thameslink, Cross Country, South Eastern and Thames franchises. It certainly made a colourful change from the blue and grey BR era! Innovation was encouraged, which led to new services such as Brighton–Rugby, Victoria–Bournemouth via Fareham, Brighton to Ashford trains, Brighton to Bristol and a 2-hourly service between Brighton/Gatwick to Reading and beyond using the new Voyager diesel multiple units (DMUs) operated by Virgin CrossCountry. Privatisation may have its critics, but there is no doubt that passenger facilities have been greatly improved over the last nineteen years, with major investment in rolling stock and station facilities. In contrast, freight has contracted to a tiny rump on the Brighton line. Wagonload freight, newspapers, mail and parcels trains have all been consigned to history, but heavy mineral and cement trains still operate to purpose-built facilities at Purley, Crawley New Yard and Ardingly. Coupled with the almost total disappearance of excursion traffic, locomotive-hauled trains are very few in number in 2013 and there are only *two* locomotives currently based on the Brighton Line – a shunter at Brighton and an electro-diesel at Stewarts Lane.

And still the Brighton line continues to develop. The East London Line from New Cross Gate has become part of Transport for London's (TfL) Overground network and been extended both north to Highbury and Islington and south to Crystal Palace and West Croydon. Operating as London Overground and including a new link between Surrey Quays and Clapham Junction over most of the erstwhile South London Line, this provides a high-frequency orbital line around the Capital operated by a fleet of new dual-voltage Class 378 units. As a result, stations between Crystal Palace/West Croydon and New Cross Gate are now operated by TfL and have been rebranded accordingly. The other major development is the extension of Thameslink to include additional destinations both south and north of the Thames. By 2018 through travel will be possible from Sussex to Bedford, Peterborough and Kings Lynn, using a new fleet of trains which will be serviced at two depots, the larger of which is currently under construction at Three Bridges. New platforms are being added at Gatwick Airport and Redhill, extra sidings installed at Selhurst depot and Brighton, East Croydon has gained a new overbridge and even minor stations such as Salfords and Balcombe are getting new waiting shelters!

1. A Historical Overview

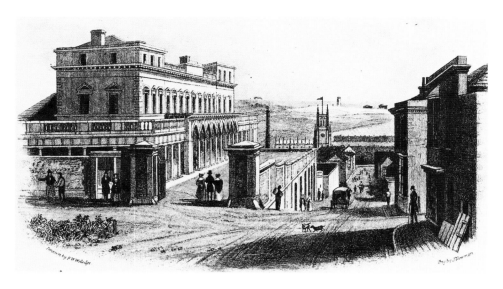

The Sussex terminus
Mocatta's station house at Brighton, *c.* 1845. Trafalgar Street slopes sharply downwards and the Downs beyond are undeveloped. (*National Railway Museum (NRM): Science and Society Picture Library*)

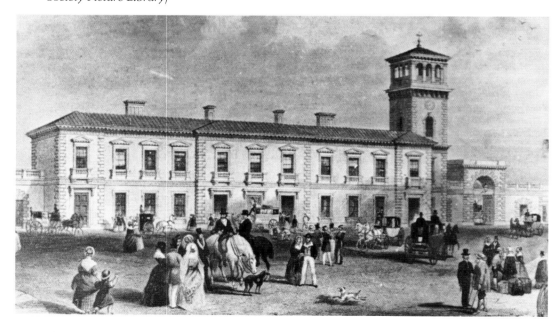

The London terminus
The print shows the 1844 London Bridge station that was replaced five years later by a larger, joint LBSCR and SER station. (*British Rail*)

A temporary London terminus

By 1844, both the SER and LCR were unhappy with arrangements with the LGR at London Bridge and opened a new terminus on the Old Kent Road, to be known as 'Bricklayers Arms'. It almost immediately became a white elephant after the SER/LGR and LBR/LCR mergers and passenger services ceased by 1852. However, it became an important freight and locomotive depot for both the SER and the LBSCR and was not closed until the 1980s. (*Wikimedia Commons*)

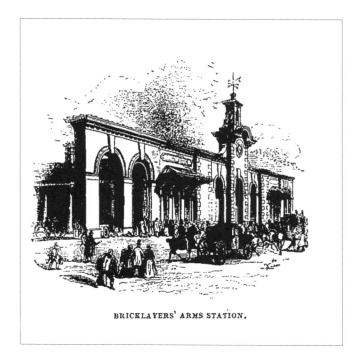

BRICKLAYERS' ARMS STATION.

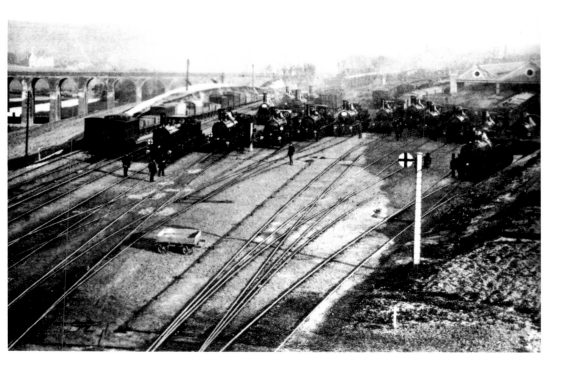

The dreaded excursionists

Locomotives wait at Brighton to take their trains back to London on Bank Holiday Monday 1872. (*Madgwick Collection*)

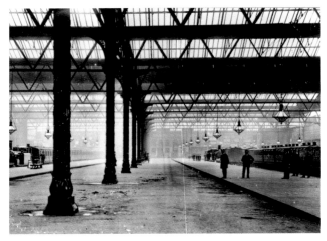

Victoria

The 'West End Twins' – Victoria was two stations in one, with the western side of the station used by the LBSCR and the eastern jointly by the LCDR and Great Western Railway. The two stations were separated by a wall, which can be seen on the right of this 1880s view, and were not amalgamated until the advent of the Southern Railway. (*Wikimedia Commons*)

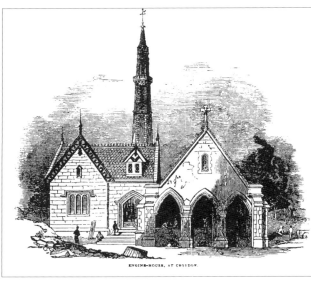

ENGINE-HOUSE, AT CROYDON.

The Atmospheric Railway

'Jolly Sailor' (Norwood Junction) in 1845, showing the gothic tower of the pumping station. This system was operated by the LCR between West Croydon and New Cross. However, the LBSCR board did not recommend its expansion and it was replaced by normal, locomotive-hauled trains by 1848. (*Wikimedia Commons*)

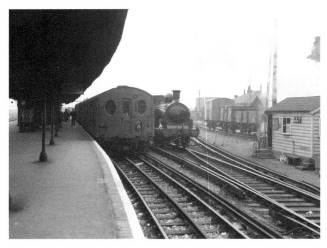

London connections – East London Line

London Transport steam and electric at New Cross Gate on 5 September 1961. A Class F unit waits on an East London Line service while preserved ex-Metropolitan E Class 0-4-4T steam loco L44 simmers alongside on a special working
(*J. J. Smith*)

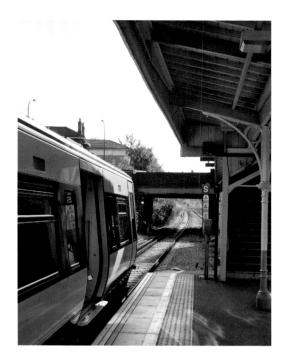

In 2012, Class 378 unit 378145 looks up the gradient with a West Croydon train on 13 October 2012. (*Simon Jeffs*)

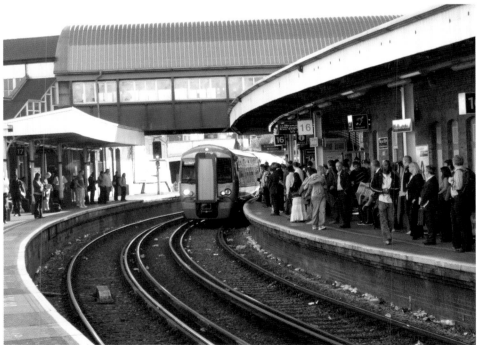

London connections – West London Line
A dual voltage (750v DC, 25kv AC) Class 377/2 unit arrives at one of the former WLER platforms at Clapham Junction on 7 August 2006 with a peak hour Milton Keynes service. (*Simon Jeffs*)

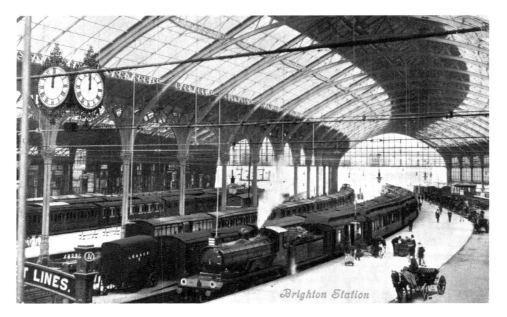

Brighton
The interior of Brighton station after the 1883 rebuild is shown in this colour postcard dating from around 1905, with a Pullman train headed by a B4 4-4-0 engine. Note the wonderful overall roof and the ornate LBSCR clock. (*Brighton Public Libraries*)

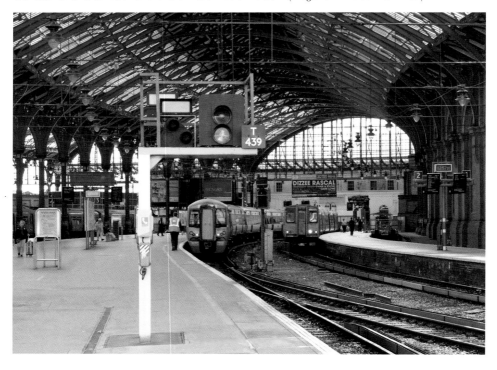

The roof is still looking wonderful in 2012, although perhaps the trains are not as glamorous! (*Simon Jeffs*)

Pullmans

An event that was to become synonymous with the Brighton line was the first appearance of Pullman cars in 1875. An all-Pullman train, The Pullman Limited Express, was introduced from 11 December 1881. This was a Sunday, and earned the train the nickname of the 'Sabbath-breaker' – a clear sign of the moral degeneracy to which the town had sunk! This colour print shows the Southern Belle, an all-Pullman train introduced in November 1908. (*NRM*)

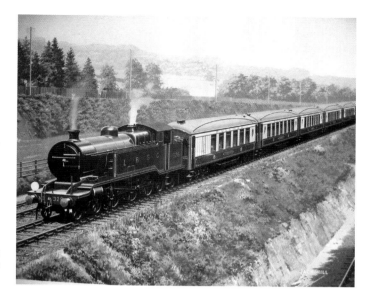

Competition

Advertising for the London & Brighton Electric Railway of 1901. The similarity between the front of the train and the Gatwick Express Class 460 units nearly a hundred years later (*below*) is striking! (*John Minnis Collection*)

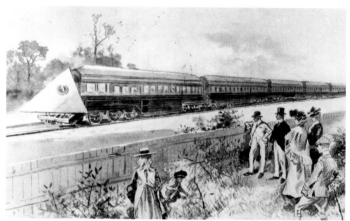

Class 460 unit 460006 passes through Horley station on 17 November 2010. The stylish Class 460 units entered service from 2002 but had a relatively short reign on the 'GATEX', the last units being withdrawn at the end of the London 2012 Olympics in August 2012. (*Peter Jones*)

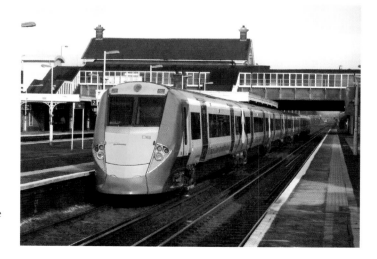

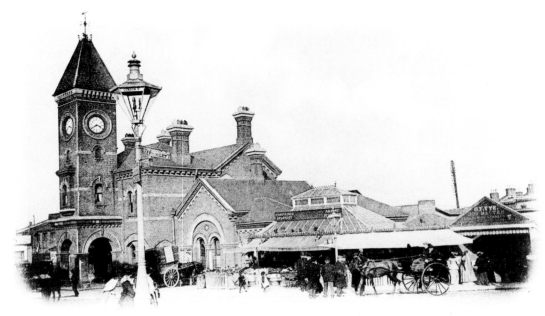

Expansion – 1

Forest Hill was supplied with a wonderfully over-the-top station to cope with its increasing commuter traffic from the 1880s. It is seen here in *c.* 1900 but was mostly destroyed during the Second World War. (*Lens of Sutton*)

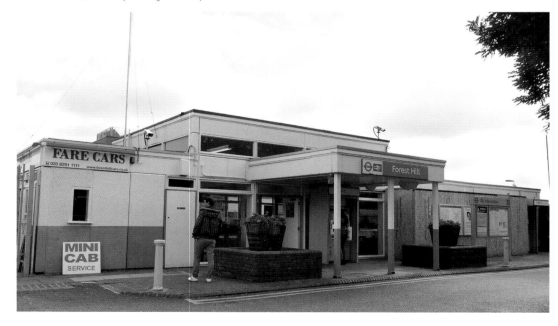

Contrast the very prosaic 1970s British Rail construction, seen here in Overground orange branding on 13 October 2012. (*Simon Jeffs*)

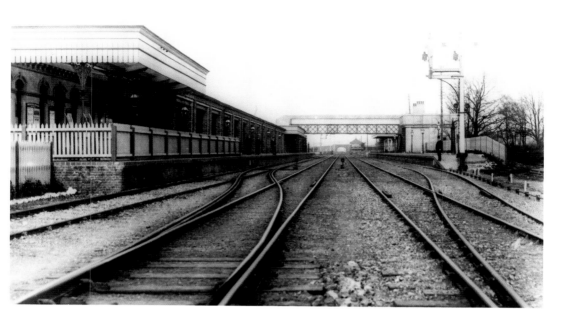

Expansion – 2:
Horley station *c.* 1885, prior to quadrupling... (*John Minnis Collection*)

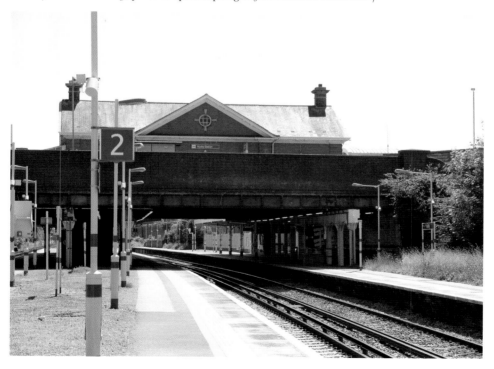

... and after. The 1905 Horley station is still serving the community today. (*Simon Jeffs*)

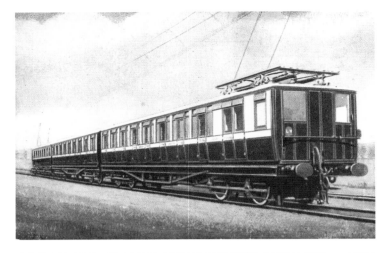

Technical innovation
One of the 1909 three-car AC electrics.
(*Dave Searle Collection*)

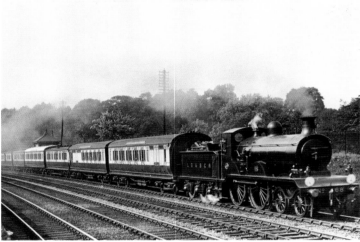

The Golden Age of the LBSCR
The Sunny South Special, a service of through carriages between Manchester, Liverpool and Birmingham via the West London Line to Brighton and Eastbourne passes Balham Intermediate signal box around 1912, with B4 4-4-0 loco No. 68 *Marlborough* in charge (*John Minnis Collection*)

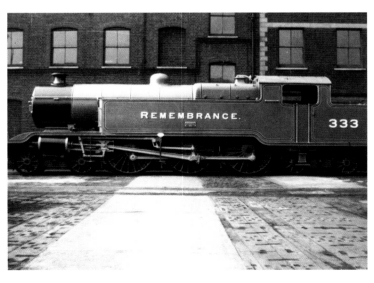

First World War
L Class loco No. 333, *Remembrance*, at Brighton Works. Below the nameplate on each side was a brass plaque with the inscription, 'In grateful remembrance of the 532 men of th L.B.&S.C.Rly. who gave their lives for their country, 1914-1919.' The loco was painted grey with black bands and white lining-out, white lettering and numerals blocked in black.
(*John Minnis Collection*))

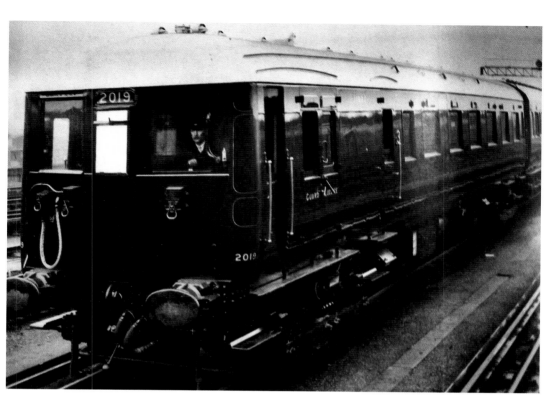

Third Rail Electrification
The motorman concentrates on his task in this posed photo of 6 Cor (later 6 Pul from 1935) unit 2019. (*SEG Archives*)

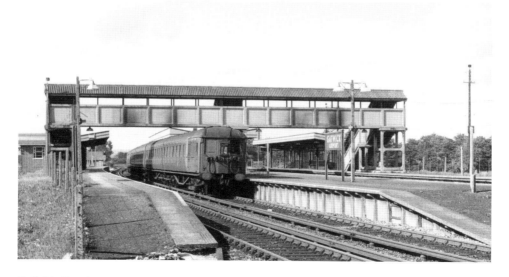

Rail-Air Services
A 4 Lav unit forms a down stopping train to Brighton at the 'old' Gatwick Airport station on 11 August 1956. (*J. H. Aston*)

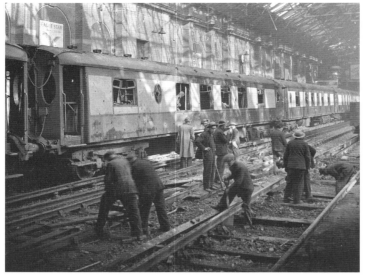

Second World War
5 Bel unit 3052 was in
the direct line of the air-
raid on Victoria, when
high explosive bombs
fell through the overall
roof on the evening
of 9 October 1940 and
damaged Pullman Cars
Audrey and *90*. (*NRM*)

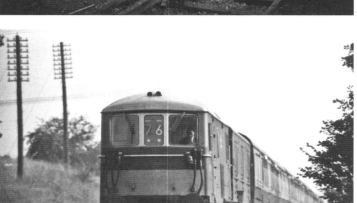

The New Order
A JB Class Electro-diesel
(later Class 73) heads an
up Newhaven boat train
composed of BR Mk 1
stock in blue and grey
livery (plus a parcels
van) near Wivelsfield in
1968. The electro-diesels
were a unique Southern
solution to haulage on
electrified and non-
electrified lines, and
many examples are still
in service.
(*Michael Baker*)

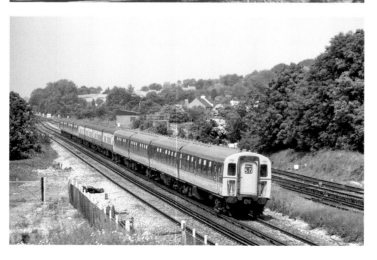

Sectorisation
The rather attractive
LSE 'Jaffa Cake' livery
is seen on two of three
Class 421 units (1710
leading) forming the
14:50 Victoria–Hastings
service on 21 June 1986
at the site of the former
Coulsdon North station,
which was swept away
in 1983. (*Chris Wilson*)

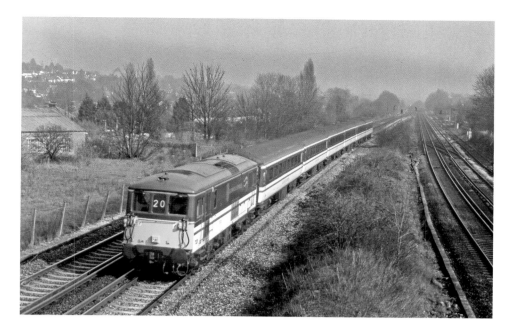

Gatwick Express
Class 73/2 loco No. 73211 passes Coulsdon (Smitham station can be glimpsed above the loco) on the 10:15 Victoria–Gatwick Airport service on 10 March 1996. (*Brian Morrison*)

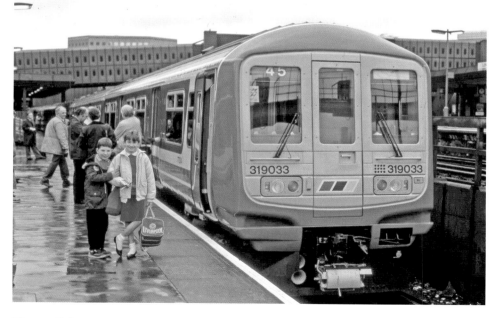

Thameslink
Thameslink services were initially solely operated by a fleet of dual voltage (25 kV AC, 750 V DC) Class 319 units. 319 033 is pictured here at London Bridge in NSE red, white and blue livery on 16 April 1988. This particular unit (with 319 031) was attempting a record run from London to Brighton. It succeeded – in 37¾ minutes! (*Don Benn*)

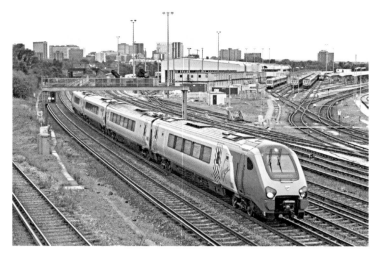

Privatisation – 1
Virgin was awarded the CrossCountry franchise and introduced a fleet of Class 221 Voyager DMUs to operate its services. 221024 *Sheffield Voyager* passes Selhurst depot on a diverted Brighton–Manchester Piccadilly service on 5 November 2005. (*Brian Morrison*)

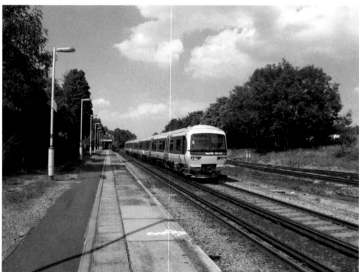

Privatisation – 2
The Thames Trains franchise, operated by the bus group Go-Ahead, used the air-conditioned Class 166 Networker Turbos on most of their Gatwick Airport–Reading services. 166203 passes Earlswood with the 13:34 Reading–Gatwick Airport service on 18 August 2005. (*Arthur Tayler*)

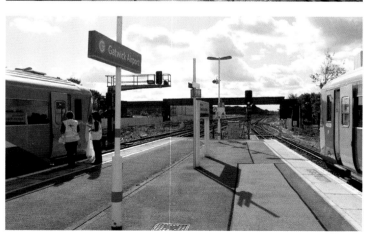

Privatisation – 3
Gatwick Express is now part of the South Central franchise operated by Govia but retains a separate identity. Services are now in the hands of the extensively-refurbished Class 442 units. Two units wait at Gatwick Airport on 19 September 2012. (*Simon Jeffs*)

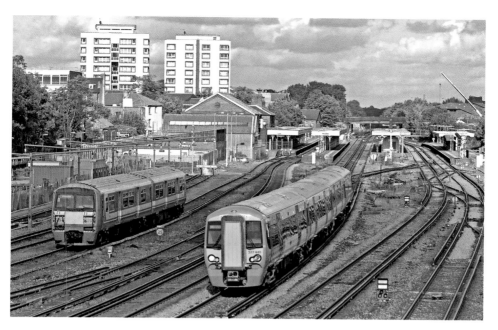

Privatisation – 4

The majority of Brighton Line services are now operated by Southern and First Capital Connect. Nearly all of the former TOCs services between London and the Sussex Coast are operated by the Class 377 Electrostar units, dating from 2001. Here, Class 377/4 377440 passes 456005, still in Network Southeast livery, at Norwood Junction. (*Brian Morrison*)

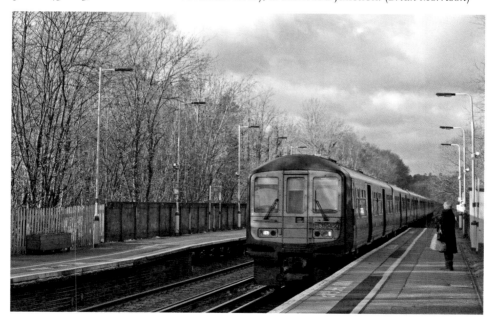

Privatisation – 5

First Capital Connect now operate the Thameslink services. 319450 arrives at Balcombe on 2 February 2013. (*Simon Jeffs*)

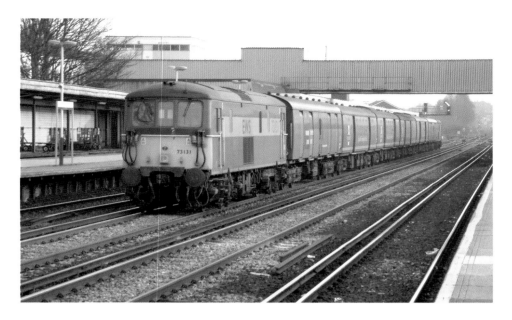

Mail

Also history are the Travelling Post Office services. Class 73 loco 73131 heads a rake of TPO vehicles at Redhill on the Willesden–Dover service on 25 March 2003. Redhill no longer handles any parcels traffic and the dedicated parcels platform (to the left) and conveyer lie unused. (*John Wills Collection © Southern Railway Net*)

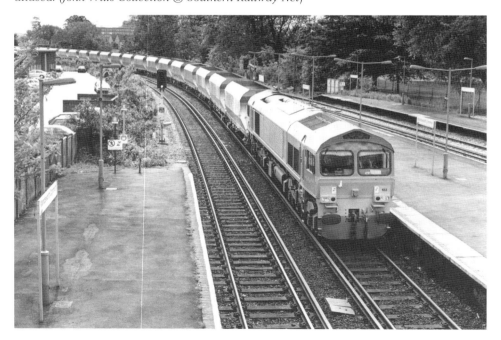

The modern railfreight image

General Motors Class 59/1 loco 59103 passes Wandsworth Common in charge of the Ardingly to Westbury stone empties on 6 June 1991. (*David Brown*)

2. London Bridge to East Croydon

London Bridge
The LBSCR side of London Bridge station was considerably altered after the opening of the SER's line to Charing Cross in 1864, while extra platforms were added by 1879, giving eleven in all. This photo shows the fine, symmetrical structure of the LBSCR station in 1882, with Terrier tanks in abundance! (*Bluebell Railway Archives*)

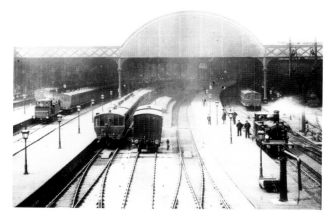

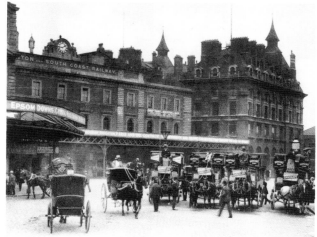

The forecourt of London Bridge LBSCR in about 1905. (*John Minnis Collection*)

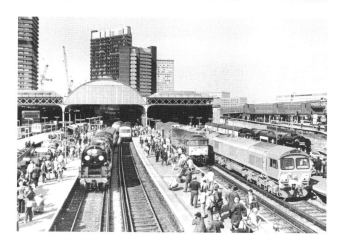

The trainshed symmetry was still apparent when Network SouthEast held an open day in 1988. (*Brian Morrison*)

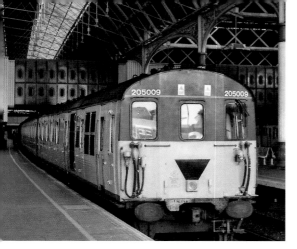
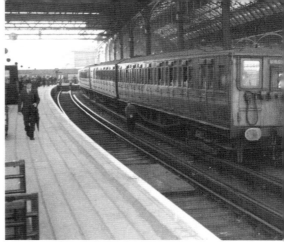

Above left: The Brighton ('Central') and SER ('East') sides were now connected by an overbridge erected as part of the 1972–8 station redevelopment. One of the Class 205 DEMUs, 205009 in Connex South Central livery, is the rear unit of the 06:56 from Uckfield on 21 June 2004. (*Don Benn*)

Above right: By 1928, nearly all of the suburban services from London Bridge had been electrified on the third rail system. This included the South London Line and eight two-car AC units were converted to DC in 1928 and classified 2 SL. Two of these venerable units, 1808 and 1801, stand inside the train shed at London Bridge prior to departure for Victoria via Peckham Rye on 17 September 1954. (*R. C. Riley Collection*)

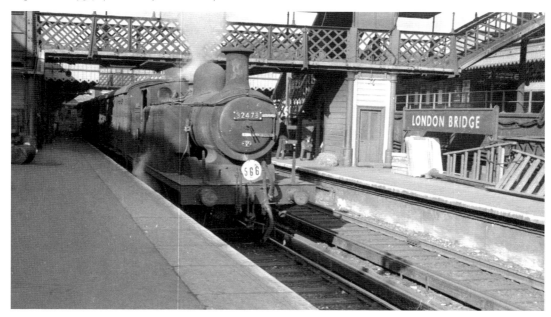

By 1909, London Bridge had twenty-one platforms. Between the Through/High Level (SER) platforms (1–4, 6/7) and the Low Level LBSCR concourse (12–22), Platforms 8–11 were used for parcels, newspaper, excursion and some peak-hour services. An E4 radial tank fusses around here in October 1959, but look closely at the number, for this is 32473, the only surviving radial tank now preserved on the Bluebell Railway. (*A. J. Wills Collection © Southern Railway Net*)

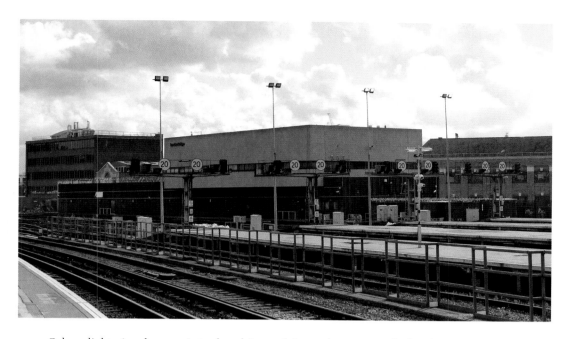

Colour light signals were introduced in 1928 in conjunction with the third rail electrification but the London Bridge area was even more comprehensively resignalled in the 1970s and all movements as far as Norwood Junction on the Brighton are now controlled by the signaling centre opened in 1973. London Bridge now (2013) has six through (1–6) and nine terminal (8–16) platforms – but all this is about to change...

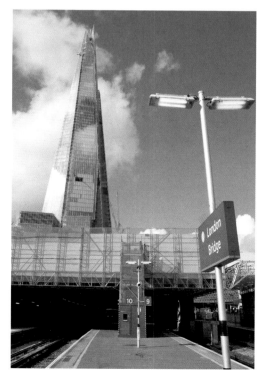

... as the station area is now undergoing the biggest redevelopment in its history in conjunction with the final part of the Thameslink Programme. As a result, the area will be a building site until 2018. The photo below shows the glass-clad Shard towering over the Brighton trainshed, which is covered in scaffolding prior to its demolition. Both views were taken on 13 October 2012. (*Simon Jeffs*)

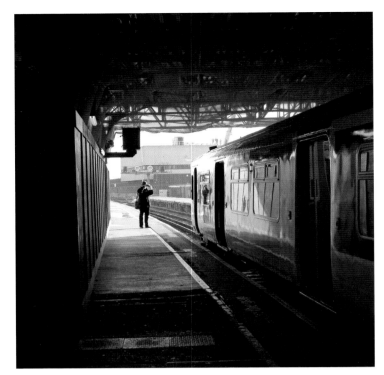

A sad day. On 8 December 2012, the last direct trains between London Bridge and Victoria on the South London Line operated, being partially replaced by an extension of the London Overground network between Surrey Quays and Clapham Junction via Denmark Hill. Unit 455825 heads out of the darkness at Platform 14 into the light. (*Simon Jeffs*)

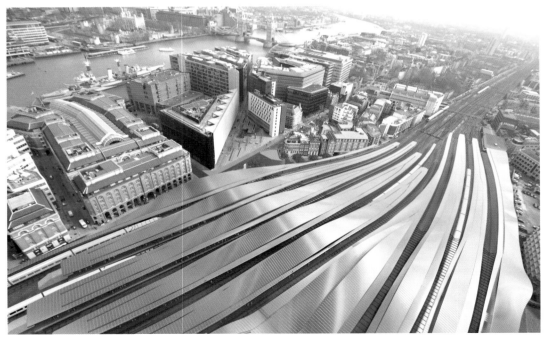

When finished in 2018, the station will have nine through platforms and six for terminating trains, using a completely rebuilt station. An artist's impression depicts the 'new' London Bridge. (*Network Rail*)

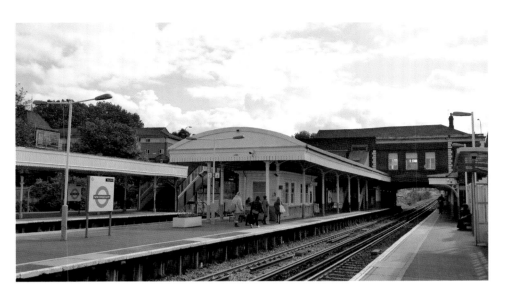

New Cross Gate

New Cross (New Cross Gate from July 1923) station opened on 1 June 1839. The New Cross area became an important junction, where the South London Line, East London Line (ELL), Bricklayers Arms branch and Deptford Wharf branch all diverged. The station was rebuilt in 1858 and 1869 and the current station layout and many of the buildings date from that time. This is a general station view taken on 13 October 2012. Note that the canopies are different on all three platforms. (*Simon Jeffs*)

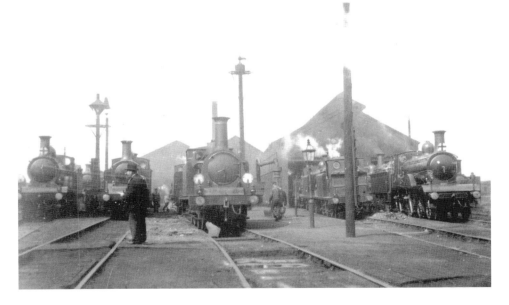

The motive power depot dates from 1839 and was to be superseded by the new shed at Norwood Junction in the 1930s but, due to the war, remained until 1951. The 'New' shed of 1882 is on the left and the Middle shed of *c.* 1864 on the right. In 1957, the whole area was replaced by EMU stabling sidings which were removed by 1988 when this work was transferred to Selhurst. (*John Minnis Collection*)

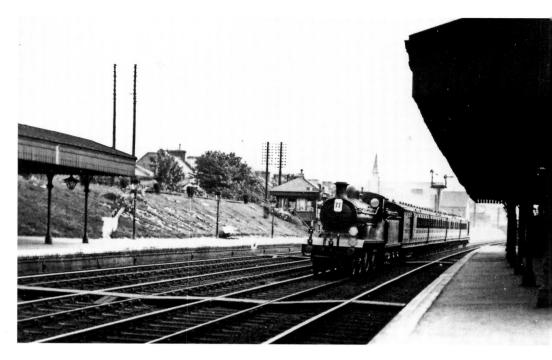

Brockley

Brockley was opened on 6 May 1871 to serve the expanding residential area around the station, a role it continues to this day. B4 4-4-0 loco B47 *Canada* heads north towards London Bridge with an express on Bank Holiday Monday, 2 August 1926. The expansive canopies have now been demolished and the station building is currently being replaced by TfL. (*H. C. Casserley*)

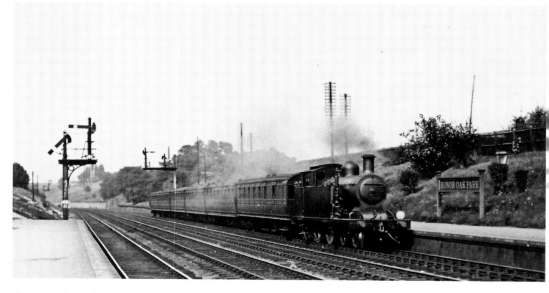

Honor Oak Park

Home from work to Honor Oak Park, opened on 1 April 1886 and partially paid for by local estate developers. An I1 4-4-2T tank runs in during August 1926. (*H. C. Casserley*)

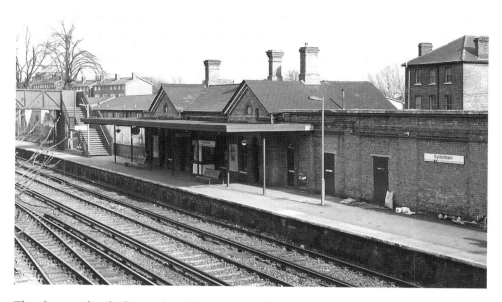

The down side platforms date from 1877 and are seen here with Network SouthEast branding on 18 February 1988. They still stand today, but with Overground branding. Platforms between here and London Bridge are currently being lengthened for ten-car trains. (*John Scrace*)

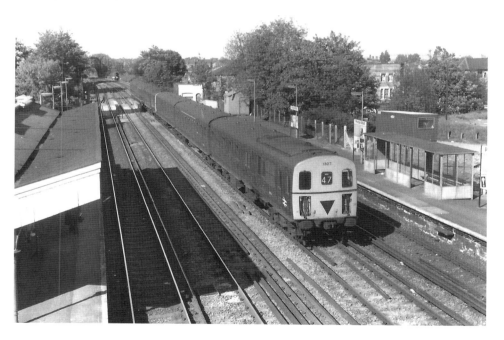

Penge West

Moving on to Penge West, two DEMUs, with 1307 leading, form the 16:40 London Bridge–Uckfield service on 14 May 1976. The down side facilities consist of a vandalized shelter. The up side buildings date from 1863. (*John Scrace*)

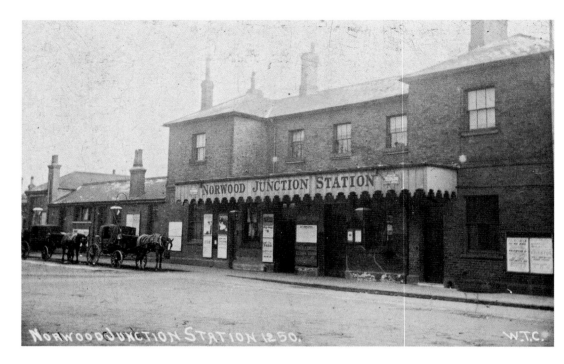

Norwood Junction

Spot the difference! Opened as Jolly Sailor (albeit a long way from the sea) in 1846, the station at Norwood Junction was moved a little way south in 1859 and the station building in the top photo provided (*Lens of Sutton*). Over 150 years later, on 13 October 2012 (bottom photo), the horses have been replaced by more modern conveyances and a new entrance provided, but the station building has barely altered. (*Simon Jeffs*)

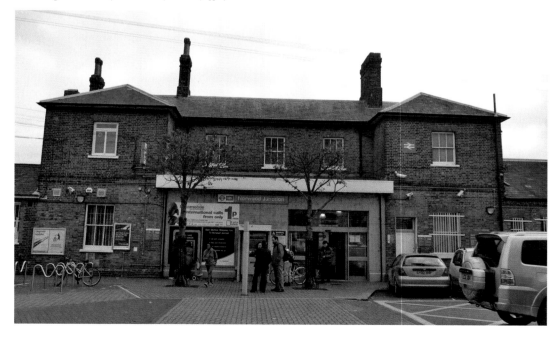

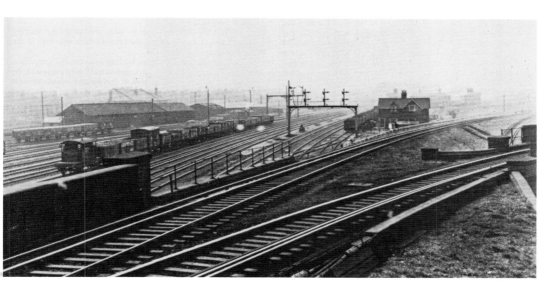

Until the 1980s, Norwood Junction was a major freight centre. Looking south, the lines to East Croydon are in the centre; that to Selhurst swings right; and those to West Croydon sweep past Railway Cottages. Norwood Yard is on the left, while Selhurst EMU depot would be further to the right in this 1937 view. (*British Rail*)

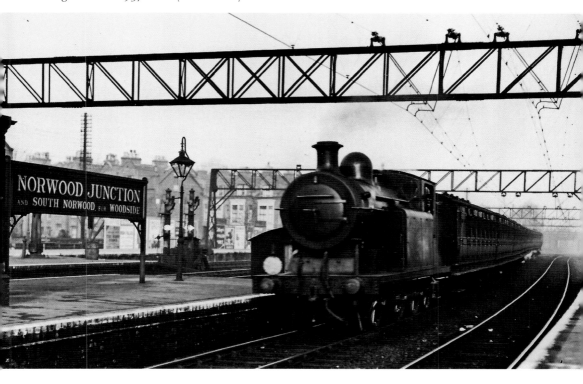

Back at the station, B576, a Class E5X 0-6-2T radial tank enters Platform 3 on 18 December 1926. The impressive running-in board reads Norwood Junction and South Norwood for Woodside, the latter being about 1 mile to the east. (*H. C. Casserley*)

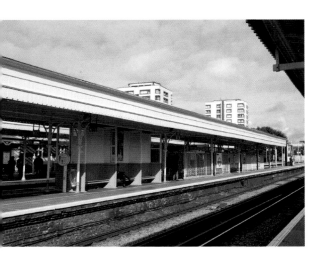

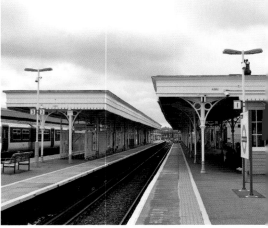

Above left: Platform 3 had changed little by October 2012, retaining its LBSCR ironwork and seating. (*Simon Jeffs*)

Above right: The whole station is a beautiful example of LBSCR architecture and well worth a visit. Platforms 1 and 2 are unusual in both serving the up slow line, although passengers normally board their trains from Platform 1. (*Simon Jeffs*)

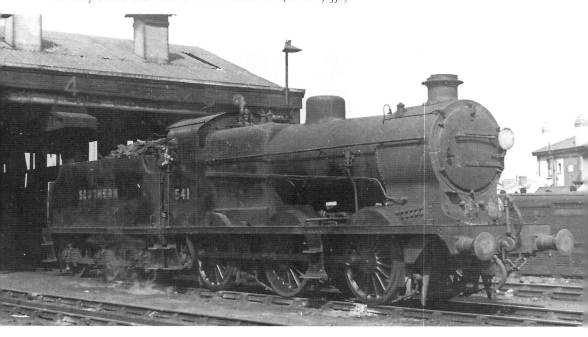

Norwood Junction shed was opened in 1935 to replace the outdated facilities at New Cross Gate. Most of the locos allocated here were used for freight work, an example being Q Class 0-6-0 541, seen on Number 4 road at the shed on 28 July 1945. The shed closed in 1964. (*H. C. Casserley*)

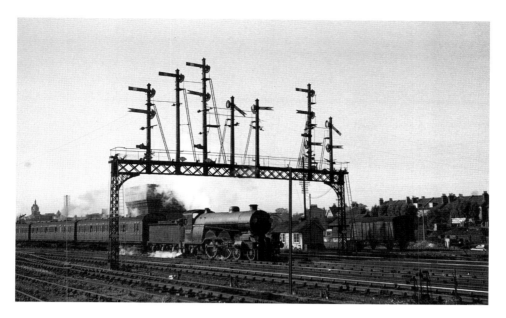

East Croydon

The famous set of LBSCR signals to the north of East Croydon station. These were removed in 1954 when the area was resignalled with colour lights. H1 Marsh Atlantic 32037 *Selsey Bill* passes on the 8.22 a.m. Lewes–London Bridge service on 5 October 1950. (*J. J. Smith*)

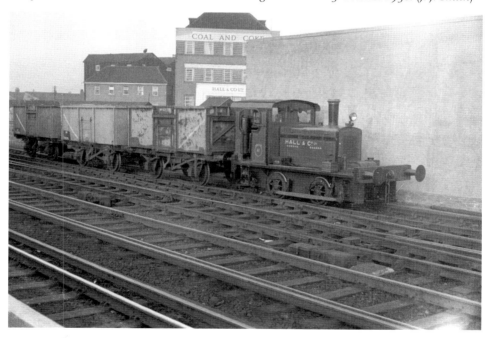

Observers (and spotters!) at East Croydon will remember the Hall & Co. yard just north of East Croydon station. A variety of industrial locos shunted here over the years and this image shows the archaic Fowler 0-4-0 diesel loco No. 10 in 1960. (*A. J. Wills Collection ©️ Southern Railway Net*)

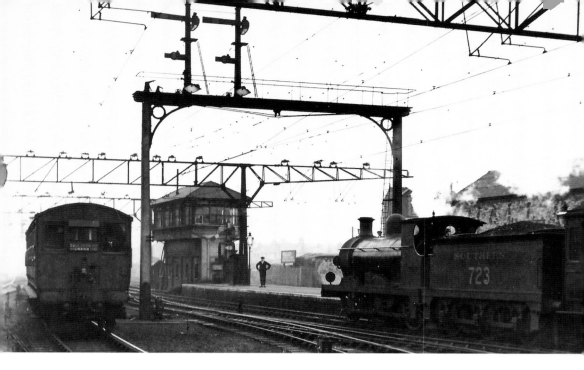

Electric trains arrived in 1925 when the AC overhead was extended to Coulsdon North, the 11 headcode on the five-car electric set on the left denoting a Victoria–Coulsdon North via Streatham Common service. Class C 0-6-0 A723 waits to depart on the right on 18 February 1926. (*H. C. Casserley*)

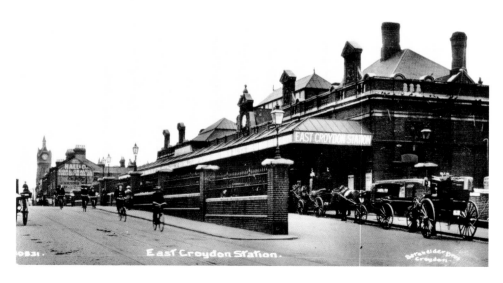

The frontage of East Croydon station on George Street is pictured around 1900. (*Wikimedia Commons*)

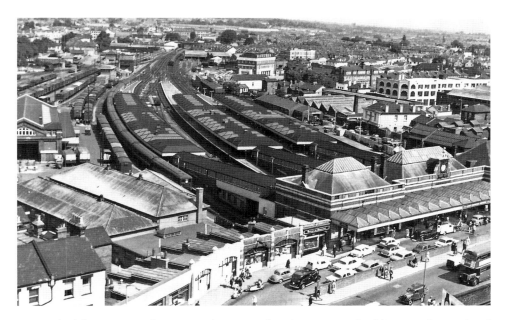

A wonderful panorama from 27 July 1963. The 1894 station buildings and associated parade of shops can be seen, with the busy goods yard to the left, a Pul/Pan rake in Platform 1 and a Sub passing Hall & Co.'s depot to the north. 'Platform 7', the Porter and Sorter public house, is the white building opposite Platform 6. No skyscrapers or trams! The goods yard closed in 1973 and the area remains a wasteland to this day. (*John Scrace*)

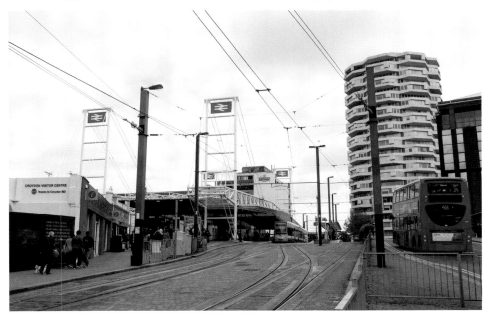

The current East Croydon station building (shown on 13 October 2012) dates from the latest rebuild of August 1992, although the shops on the left still date from 1894/5 (behind the modern façades). Excellent connections can be made with the Croydon Tramlink system to New Addington, Beckenham Junction, Elmers End and Wimbledon and local buses. (*Simon Jeffs*)

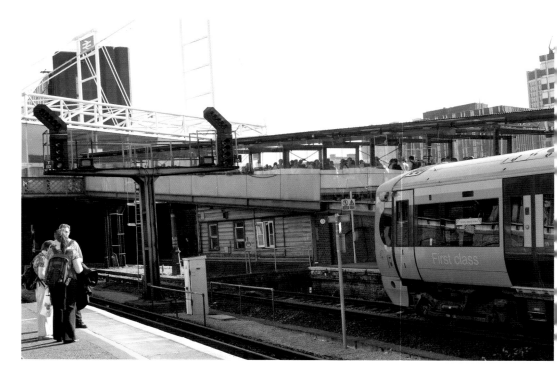

All three-island platforms now have a full range of facilities and the entrance/exit ramps have been reclad. Remnants of the Victorian station can still be seen beneath the ramps, though. A Class 377 Electrostar unit waits to depart with a Brighton service on 26 July 2012. (*Simon Jeffs*)

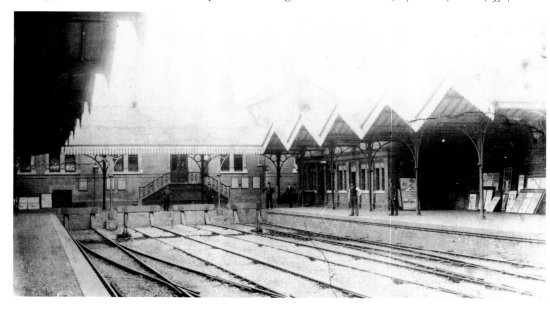

Before leaving Croydon, let us not forget the fourth Croydon station (after East, West and South). This is Central Croydon Station, opened in 1868 and closed by 1890. The present town hall and gardens now occupy the site. (*Croydon Libraries*)

3. Victoria–Selhurst

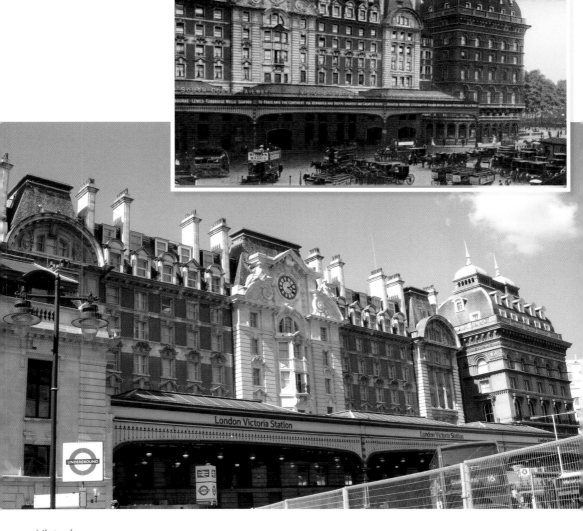

Victoria

Inset: A view of the Brighton station from about 1911. The Grosvenor Hotel is on the right. (*John Minnis Collection*)

The frontage has altered little since 1910. The bus station was added in 1926 and extra entrances to the Underground provided when the Victoria Line opened in March 1969. Currently (2013), the Underground section is being massively expanded and rebuilt to provide extra capacity and the area around the station is a building site. This view, from 13 June 2012, was taken from the top deck of a No. 36 bus! (*Simon Jeffs*)

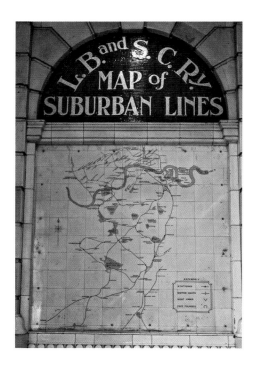

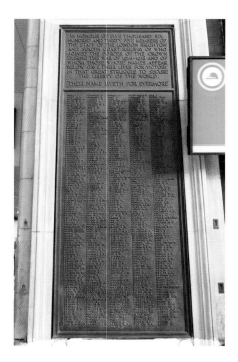

Above left and right: Unlike London Bridge, Victoria retains many interesting architectural features dating from Edwardian days. Two to look out for are the tiled wall maps (in the exit passage by Marks & Spencers) depicting the LBSCR Suburban Lines (*above left*) and the main lines; and (*above right*) the memorial to the 523 LBSCR employees who lost their lives in the First World War. (*Simon Jeffs*)

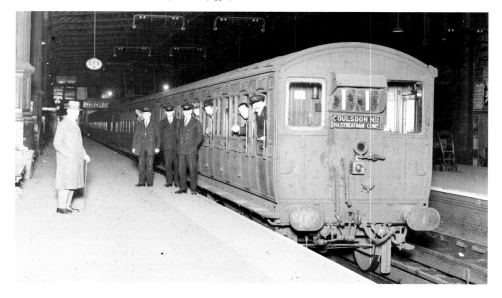

End of the 'Elevated Electric'. The last AC EMU departs Victoria for Coulsdon North at 12.30 a.m. on 22 September 1929. Note that the conductor rails are already in place for the DC EMUs, having been used for some months already. (*NRM*)

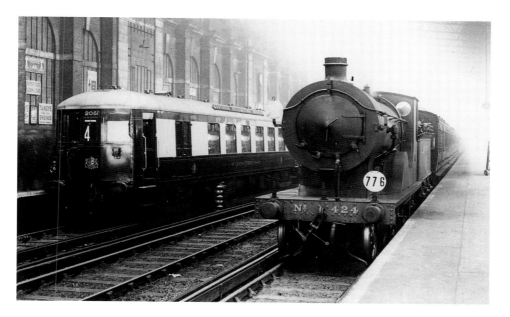

On the first day of main line electric services to Brighton, 1 January 1933, the Southern Belle, now formed of new 5 Bel units, waits at Platform 17 while an ex-LSWR Drummond S11 awaits departure with a train over the yet to be electrified Mid-Sussex route. The Southern Belle became the more-familiar Brighton Belle from 29 June 1934. (*NRM*)

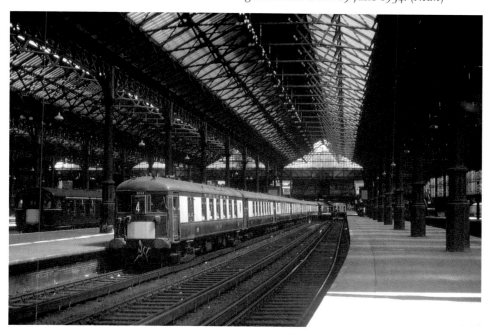

This view, taken on 13 June 1968, demonstrates the enormous length of the Brighton side platforms. A train could depart from the 'Town' end of the platforms and, by using the centre track, overtake a second train parked at the 'Country' end. 5 Bel unit 3052 departs on the 11:00 Brighton Belle service, flanked by a 4 Cig and an Oxted 3D DEMU. (*John Scrace*)

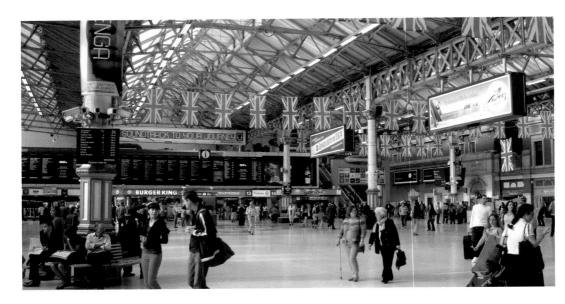

The Brighton side concourse still retains the ridge and furrow roof design over the train shed seen in the previous photos. Two extra platforms were provided in 1983, making nineteen in all. This allowed Platforms 13 and 14 to be dedicated to the non-stop Gatwick Express service that commenced the following year. The gate line under the train indicators gives access to Platforms 9–14, Platforms 15 to 19 are tucked away to the right of the escalators. The station, seen on 13 June 2012, is decorated for the Queen's Diamond Jubilee and the London Olympic and Paralympic Games. (*Simon Jeffs*)

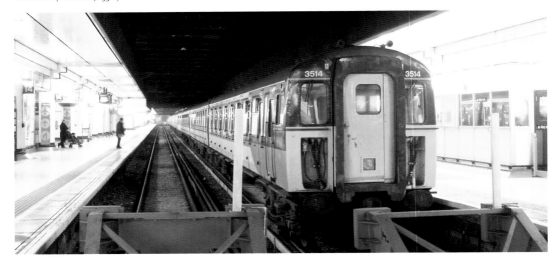

Developers have long coveted stations for commercial development. British United Airways opened terminal facilities that partially obscured platforms 15/16 (as was) in 1962, and a massive concrete raft to house additional facilities for airport passengers and the Victoria Place shopping centre was built in the 1980s. This has had the effect of completely obscuring Platforms 15–19, which, despite bright lighting, white terrazzo floor tiles and white platform buildings, now provides a gloomy and claustrophobic environment. The EMU is Class 423 No. 3514 and the date is 3 December 2003. (*Tony Rispoli*)

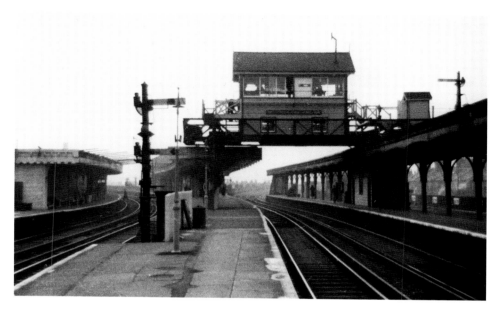

Battersea Park

At Battersea Park station, the South London Line (*left*) and Brighton Main Line (*right*) diverge. The area was formerly signalled by this rather splendid signalbox straddling the Brighton slow lines in this 1936 view. (*David Brown Collection*)

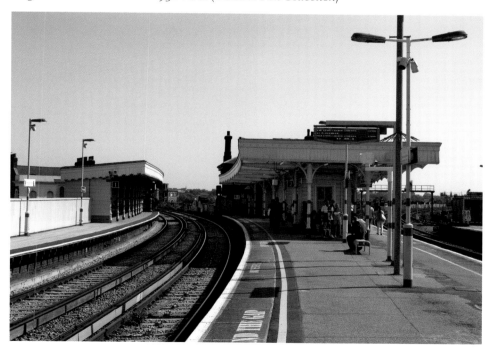

Taken in almost the same position on 26 July 2012, the box was closed in October 1979 and the canopies on the up fast platform have been removed. Along with Norwood Junction, this is probably the best example of an LBSCR station today on the Brighton Line. (*Simon Jeffs*)

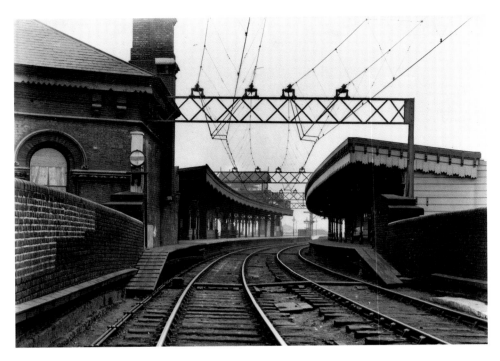

Entering the station from the South London Line, the AC overhead is prominent in this 1909 view. (*R. C. Riley Collection*)

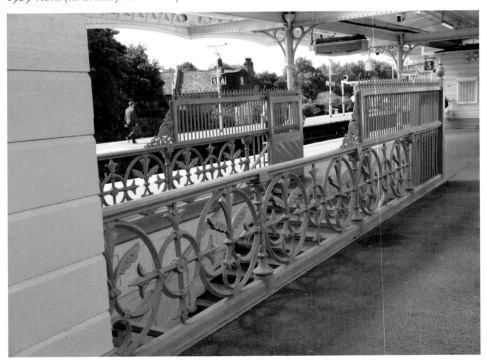

Fine ironwork on platforms 3 and 4...

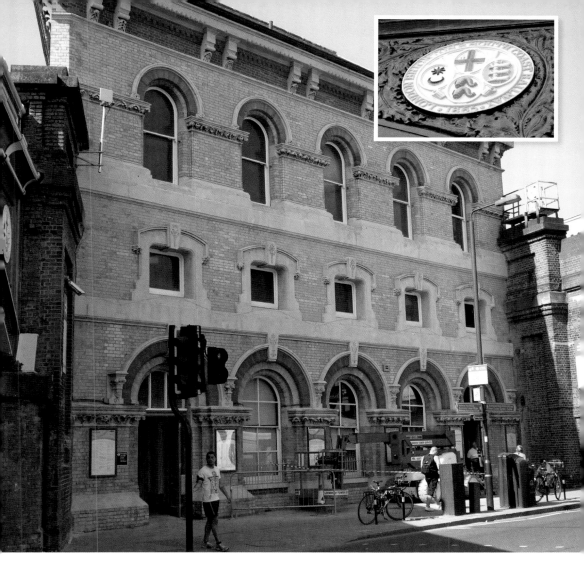

... and the beautifully-restored station frontage. Note the LBSCR coat of arms on the bridge spandrel (*insert*). (*Simon Jeffs*)

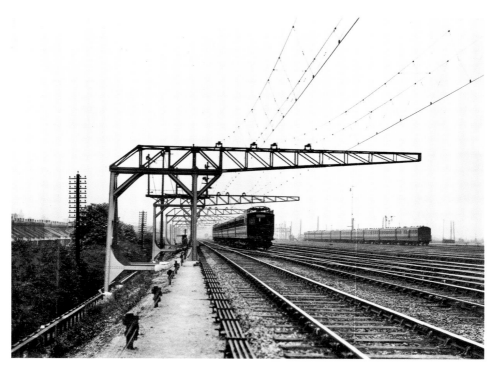

Clapham Junction
Pouparts junction was where the lines to Victoria and Waterloo diverged. An up AC electric train from Crystal Palace to Victoria is seen in this 1912 view. (*R. C. Riley Collection*)

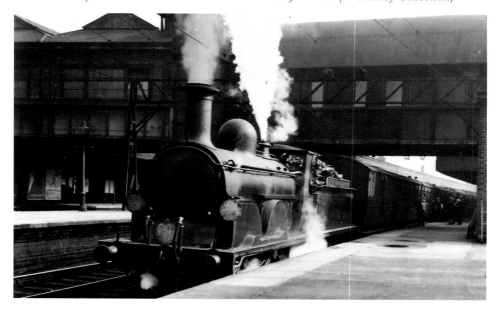

Traditional LBSCR traction in the shape of B1 Gladstone No. B179 *Sandown* waits with a Bognor Regis train on 10 July 1927. Note the differing styles of construction employed by the LSWR (*left*) and LBSCR (*right*) on the overbridge. (*H. C. Casserley*)

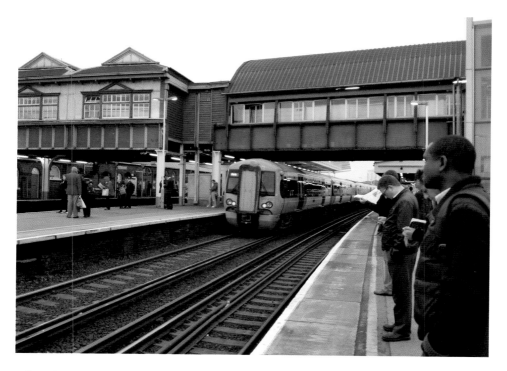

Taken from the same position on 23 October 2012, a Class 377 unit departs for Victoria while commuters wait for the next train towards East Croydon. The overbridge remains but lifts have been provided. (*Simon Jeffs*)

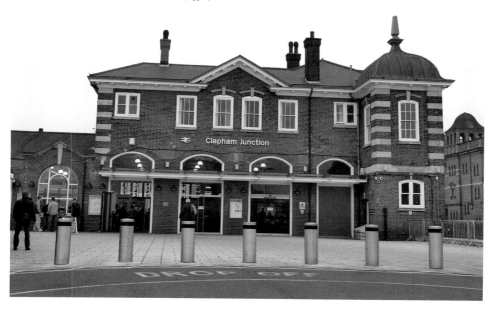

The LBSCR provided a fine station building on St Johns Hill in 1910 giving direct access to the overbridge. This was replaced in 1987 by a new booking hall located in The Junction shopping mall, further down St Johns Hill. The original 1910 building re-opened in 2010. (*Simon Jeffs*)

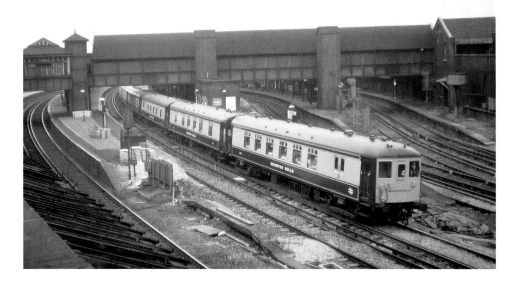

Back on the platforms, a Brighton Belle service, with 5 Bel unit 3053 leading, sweeps south on 16 June 1969. The full extent of the LBSCR overbridge is visible, while a water column for steam locos still stands on Platform 17. (*John Scrace*)

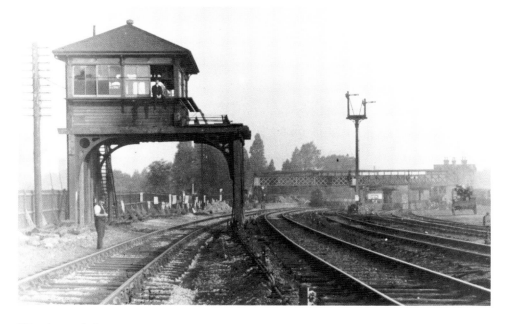

Wandsworth Common
The new station at Wandsworth Common (opened in November 1869) replaced that at New Wandsworth. The signalbox pictured closed in 1907 and was replaced by a new box when the widening work was completed. (*John Minnis Collection*)

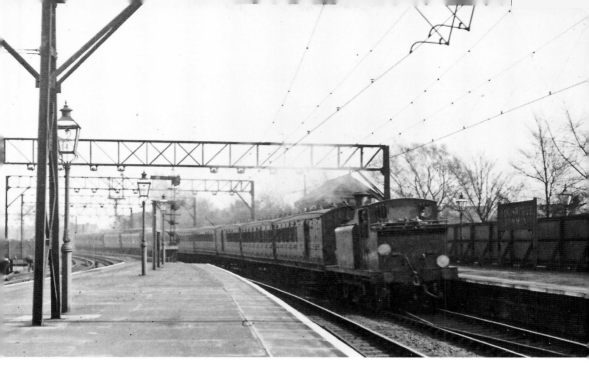

E4 0-6-2T Radial Tank B515 heads north under the AC wires with a lengthy train of empty coaching stock on 9 April 1928. (*H. C. Casserley*)

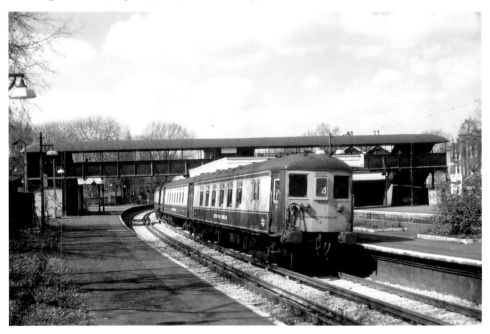

The 11:00 Victoria–Brighton Brighton Belle heads south on a lovely spring day in the last month of its life, 6 April 1972. (*John Scrace*)

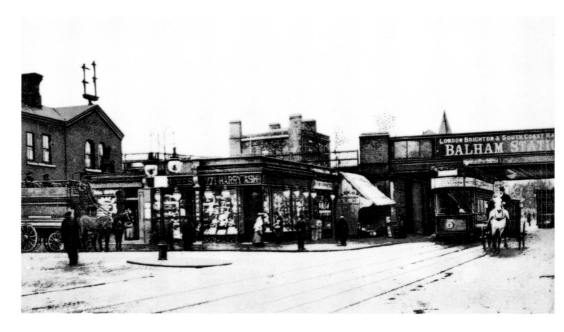

Balham

'Balham – Gateway to the South' (as immortalized by Peter Sellers). The High Street, complete with both electric and horse-drawn trams, is pictured in this view from 1908. (*A. J. Wills Collection* © *Southern Railway Net*)

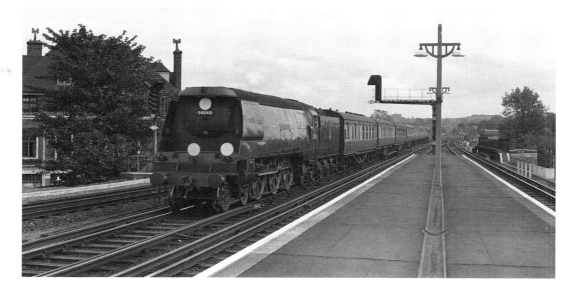

Looking south, the older line to Crystal Place continues straight ahead, past the Streatham Hill EMU servicing facility. The newer line to East Croydon curves to the right. Brighton Works-built West Country 4-6-2 loco 34046 *Braunton* enters with empty coaching stock on 19 July 1957. The rather shabby station had been extensively rebuilt with two wide island platforms in 1954. The new (1952) Balham signal box, located in the V of the junction, is in the distance. It was superseded by the Victoria ASC in 1981. (*J. J. Smith*)

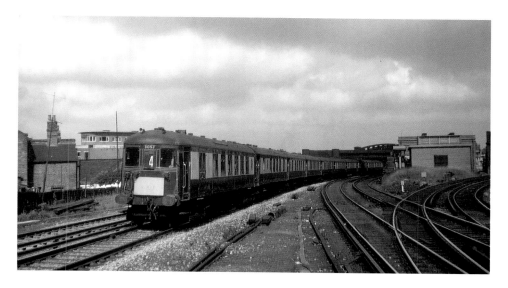

Streatham Common

North of Streatham Common is an extensive series of junctions where the line from Sutton to London Bridge crosses the Brighton Main Line. The chord to the right connects the BML slow lines to the London Bridge line, while, just beyond the signal box in the background, a further spur connects the line from Sutton to the BML fast lines. Further back towards Balham, another line leaves the BML slow lines and connects to the Sutton direction. These last two chords were once used for the fast Victoria–Bognor Regis/Portsmouth services via Sutton, Dorking and Horsham but, since 1978, these trains have been diverted via Gatwick Airport. A Brighton Belle passes on 13 September 1968. (*John Scrace*)

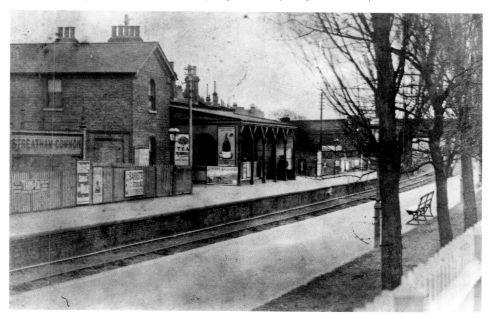

The station was opened on 1 December 1862, and is seen here prior to the 1900–03 quadrupling project. (*John Minnis Collection*)

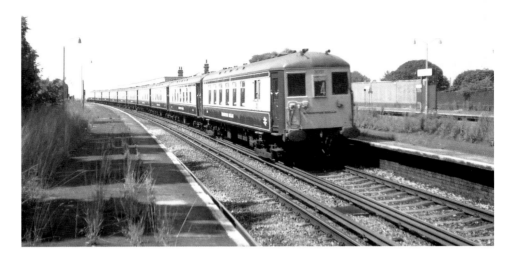

Norbury

Norbury is probably one of the least-photographed locations in this survey. Thanks are due to John Scrace for this study of the Brighton Belle on 30 July 1969. The station once boasted extensive canopies on all platforms. Those on the up fast have been removed, but the station was extensively refurbished in 2011. (*John Scrace*)

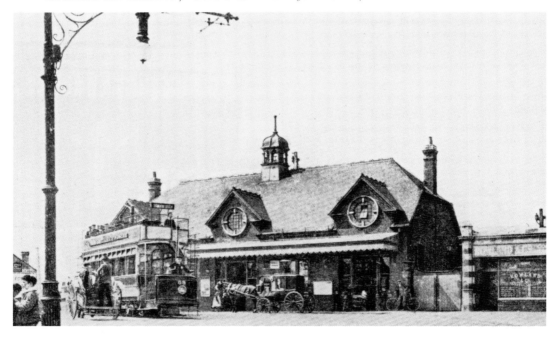

Thornton Heath

The station buildings on the overbridge are seen around 1905. The eclectic style is similar to those at Norbury, Streatham Common and Selhurst. (*Lens of Sutton*)

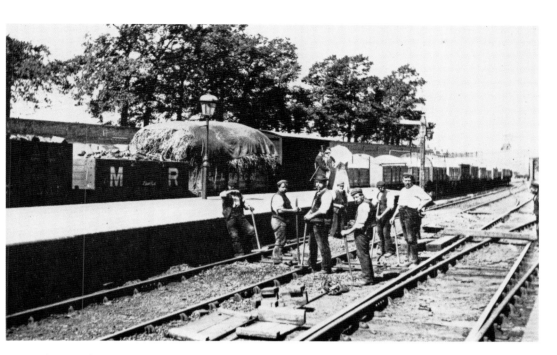

'The Sunday Gang' are putting in a new crossover at Thornton Heath on 12 August 1900. (*R. C. Riley Collection*)

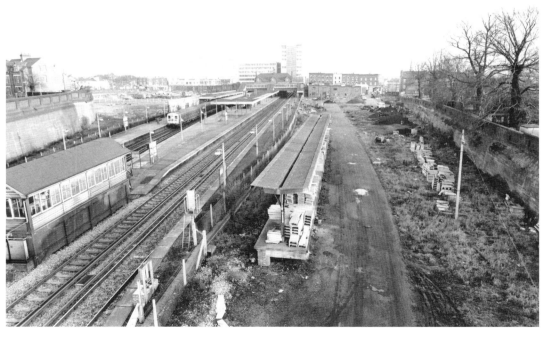

The goods yards closed in October 1968 and are seen being dismantled. Croydon's skyscrapers loom on the horizon. (*Graham Feakins*)

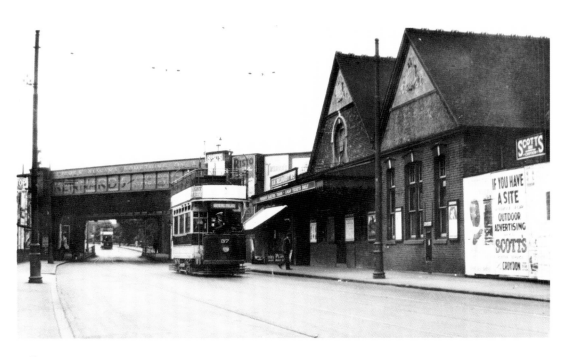

Selhurst
Croydon Corporation trams rumble past the station in this *c.* 1930 view. (*John Minnis Collection*)

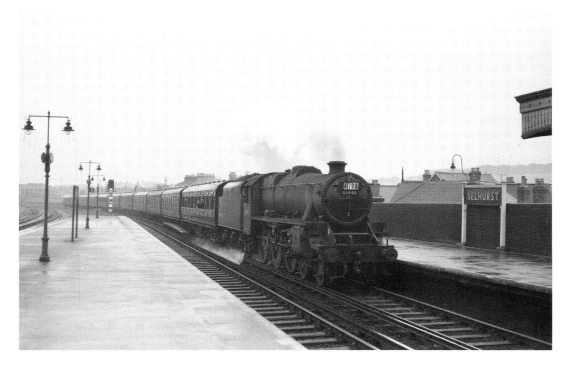

Black 5 4-6-0 Loco no. 45540 arrives at Selhurst on 26 November 1960 on a football special. Crystal Palace play at Selhurst Park, close to the station. (*J. J. Smith*)

The station was nicely refurbished in 2011. Note the fence along the island platform separating the slow and fast lines. These were also installed at Purley, Purley Oaks, South Croydon, and from Selhurst to Wandsworth Common (except Balham) during 2012 to prevent suicides. (*Simon Jeffs*)

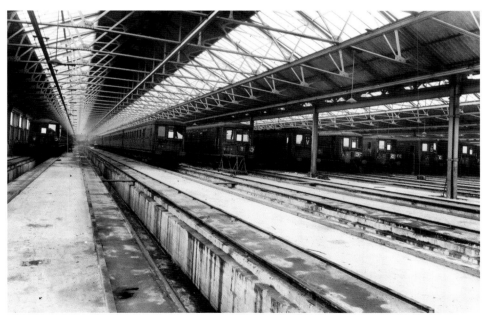

Selhurst was chosen as the site for the second servicing depot (after Peckham Rye on the SLL) for the AC overhead electrics. From 1928, the facility was converted to house third-rail DC electrics. Since then, the depot has expanded massively and is now Southern's major EMU maintenance centre. (*J. J. Smith*)

4. South Croydon to Brighton

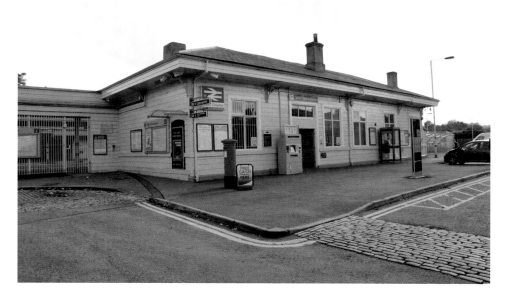

South Croydon
The charming station building, like East Croydon, dates from the 1894/5 quadrupling and retains most of its LBSCR architecture. (*Lester Hayes*)

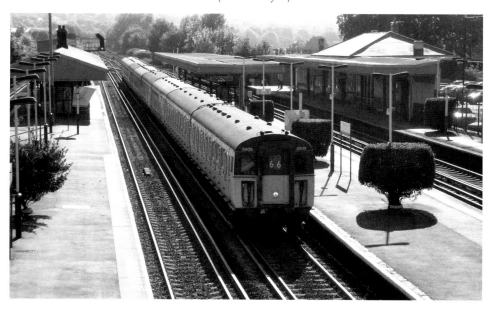

Until around 2005, the station was distinguished by some fine topiary which, unfortunately, has now been removed. 4 Vop unit 3906 is seen passing. (*Colin Scott-Morton*)

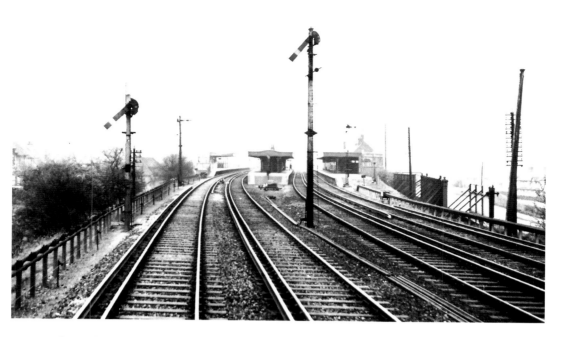

Purley Oaks
Another rarely photographed suburban station, seen on 29 September 1937.
(*H. C. Casserley*)

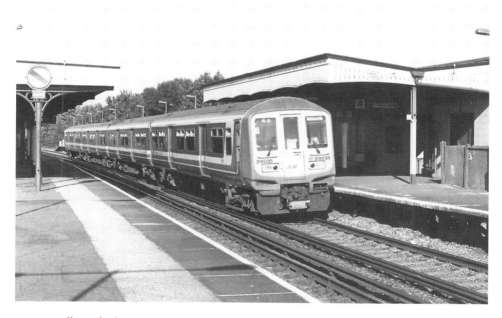

319035 calls with the 14:26 Luton–Purley service on 19 September 1989; passengers must use a subway to access the ticket office on Platforms 2/3. (*John Scrace*)

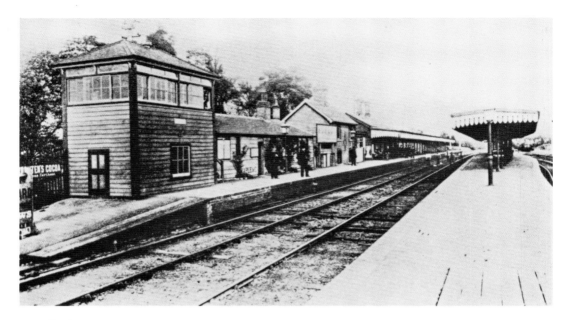

Purley

The station is seen *c.* 1890, before the quadrupling. (*Pamlin Prints*)

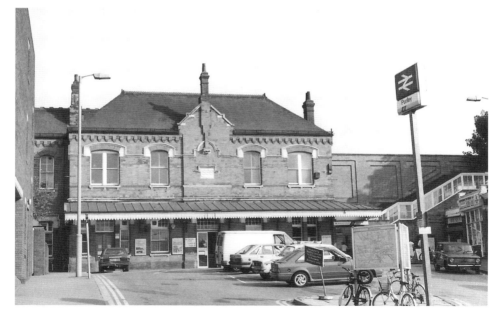

The main station buildings are on the up side and date from 1899. (*John Scrace*)

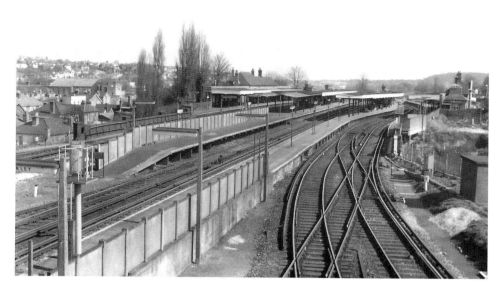

A view across the station in 1976. The fast lines are on the far left, followed by the slow and, on the right, the Caterham and Tattenham Corner lines. (*John Scrace*)

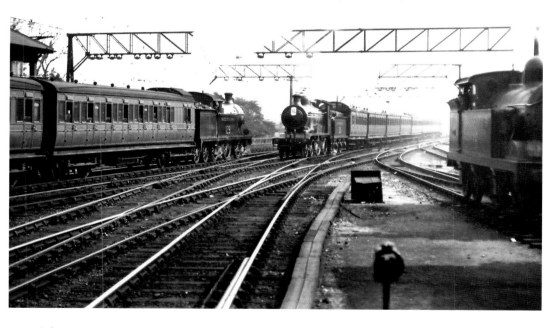

A busy scene on 2 August 1926 sees ex-SECR J Class 0-6-4T A129 and ex-LBSCR B2X 4-4-0 B210 passing, with H Class 0-4-4T A16 shunting. (*H. C. Casserley*)

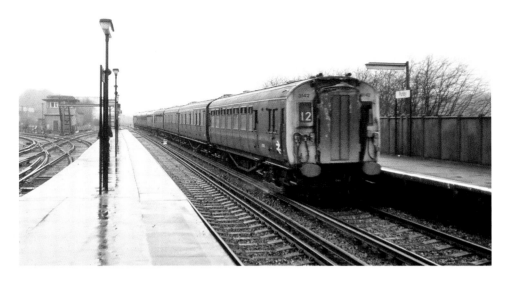

Two 4 Cor units rattle through Purley on a Brighton–Victoria semi-fast service on a wet 6 February 1972. The leading unit, 3142, has been preserved by the Southern Electric Group and is currently located at the East Kent Railway, Shepherdswell, Kent. Purley signalbox is in the background and beyond that, the SER loco shed which serviced steam locos between 1898 and 1928. It is now a training centre for railway staff. (*Bryan Rayner*)

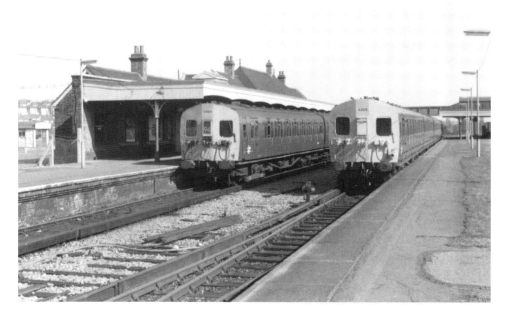

Coulsdon North
In November 1899, the LBSCR opened its new station at Coulsdon, named Stoats Nest for Coulsdon and Cane Hill, with two platforms on the new Quarry Line and two for terminating local services from London. After several more name changes, Coulsdon North was settled on by August 1923. Two 4 Sub units, 4694 and 4289, rest on 28 March 1976. (*David Brown*)

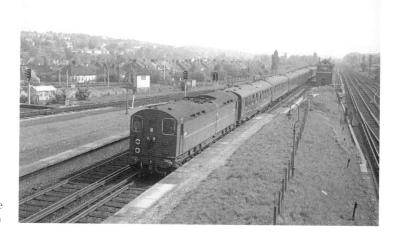

Thirteen years earlier, on 26 May 1963, the 09:25 Victoria–Newhaven Harbour boat train, with 'Hornby' loco 20003 in charge, enters Platform 4 on the fast lines. Smitham station (on the Tattenham Corner Branch) is in the background. (*Don Benn*)

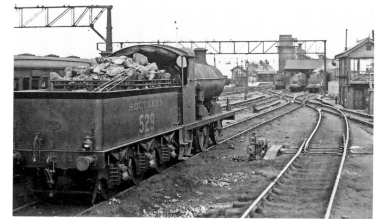

Between 1900 and 1928, a shed was provided at Coulsdon North, just beyond platforms 2/3. C2X 0-6-0 loco B529 waits its next duty on 12 February 1928. (*H. C. Casserley*)

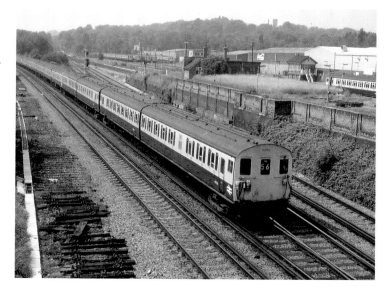

No platforms were provided on the slow lines, trains calling at Coulsdon South instead. 4 Cap unit 3202 and two Class 421 units, 7368/99, head north with a train from Bognor Regis on 18 July 1983. The front unit is joining the link line from the slow to fast (Quarry) lines. The siding to the left leads to Hall & Co.'s quarry. South of the station, twelve carriage sidings were provided. (*Alex Dasi-Sutton*)

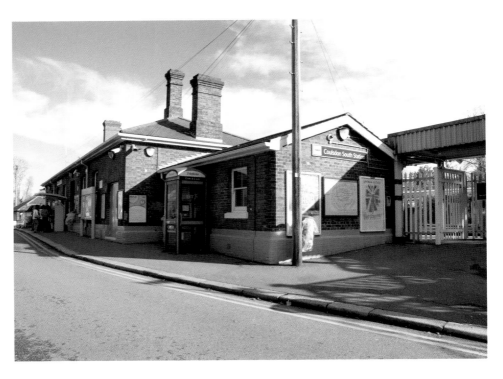

Coulsdon South
Opened by the SER as Coulsdon in October 1889, it was finally renamed Coulsdon South at the same time as Coulsdon North, in August 1923. The original station buildings are still in use and are seen on 2 November 2012. (*Lester Hayes*)

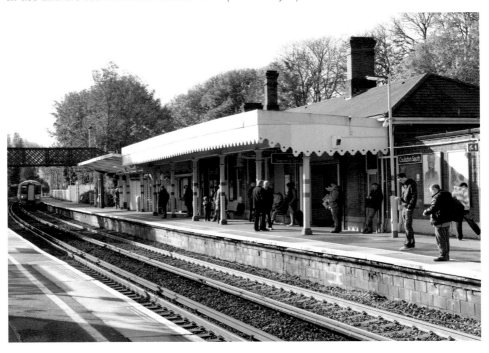

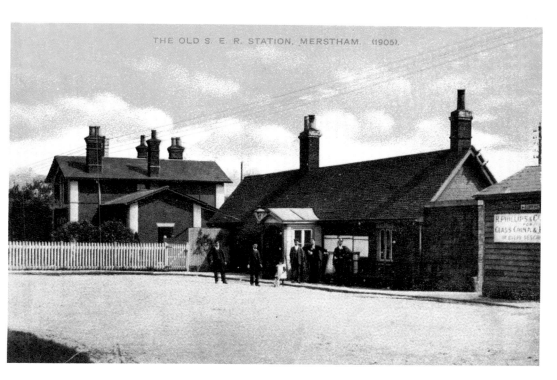

Merstham
The postcard provides the date for this view of Merstham station – 1905. (*A. J. Wills Collection © Southern Railway Net*)

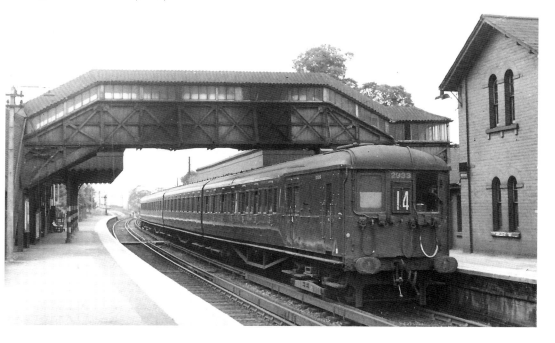

Forty-one years later, 4 Lav No. 2933 arrives with a Victoria service. (*H. C. Casserley*)

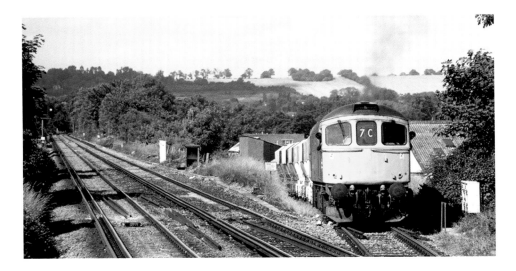

Holmethorpe

At Holmethorpe, between Redhill and Merstham, a siding gave access to the British Industrial Sand works. These were shunted by a variety of industrial locos that could be glimpsed from the Quarry line. Fully loaded sand trains were hauled by mainline locos, such as Crompton 33004, toiling up the gradient on 10 July 1978. The works have now been completely swept away and replaced by a housing estate grouped around a lake. (*Chris Wilson*)

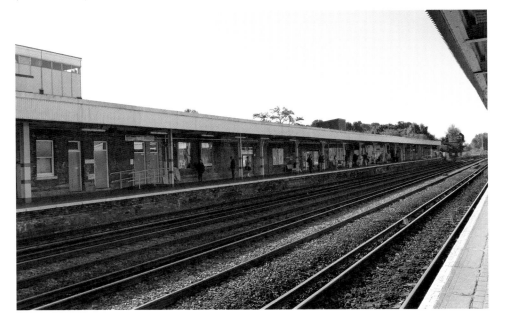

Redhill

The SER side of Redhill (now Platform 3), pictured on 19 September 2012. The station was opened on its present site in April 1844, when it was known as Reigate, and the visible brickwork on the down platform buildings dates from the rebuild in 1848. It remained an SER station until the grouping in 1923. (*Simon Jeffs*)

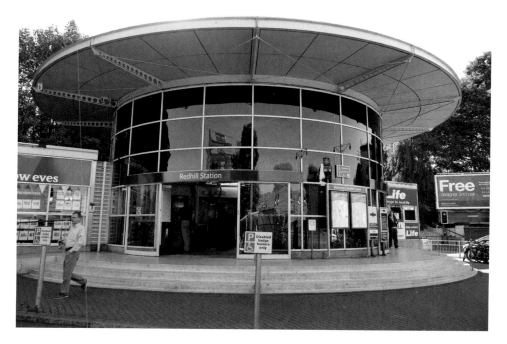

Although some SER architecture remains, the booking hall is an ultra-modern structure, seen here on 19 September 2012. (*Simon Jeffs*)

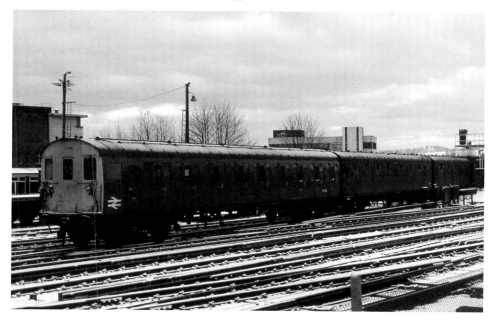

Between 1964 and 1978, the hybrid 'Tadpole' DEMUs monopolised workings between Tonbridge, Redhill and Reading. 1204 leaves Redhill on a snowy 26 January 1979. (*John Atkinson*)

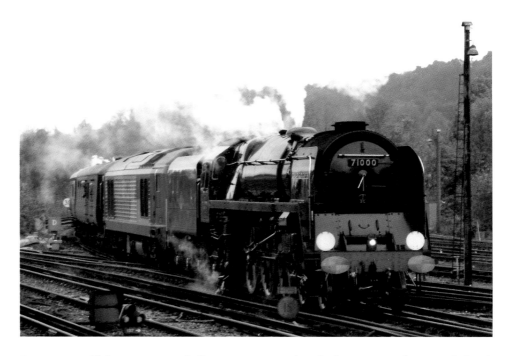

Steam can still be seen at Redhill. 4-6-2 71000 *Duke of Gloucester*, with 67022 behind, arrives at Redhill with a Venice-Simplon Orient Express Surrey Hills Dining Special on 5 November 2010. (*Peter Jones*)

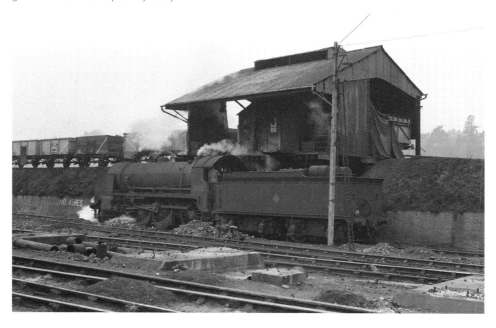

A steam depot was located between the Brighton and Tonbridge line. A Class H15 4-6-0 goods engine is seen under the coaling stage on 19 March 1960. The shed closed to steam in June 1965, but was used to stable diesel locos and DMUs until the mid-1990s. (*J. J. Smith*)

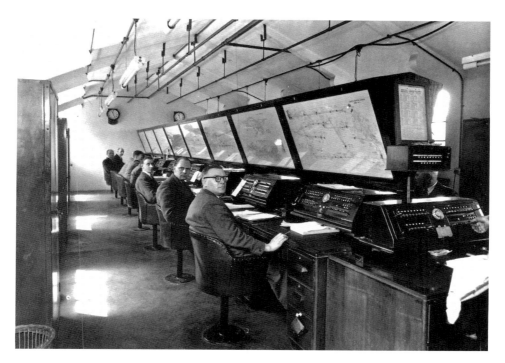

A Control centre (the London Control District Superintendent's Office) was also located at Redhill and is seen on 9 May 1950. (*Robin Levett*)

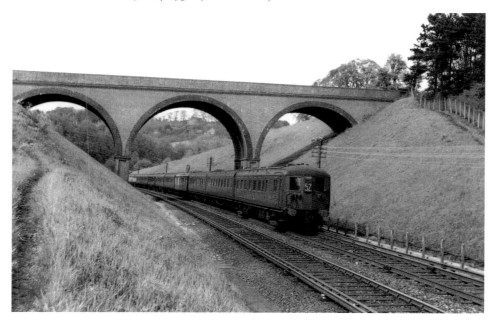

Quarry Line
The location between Merstham (Quarry) and Redhill (Sand) tunnels was often used for publicity shots. 6 Pul 3009 heads south with an Eastbourne train in the 1950s. (*J. H. Aston*)

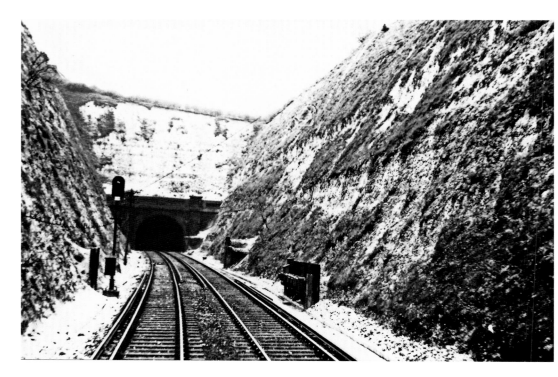

Merstham (Quarry) tunnel is seen in 1937. The chalk cutting sees frequent rock falls and is now coated in protective netting. (*H. C. Casserley*)

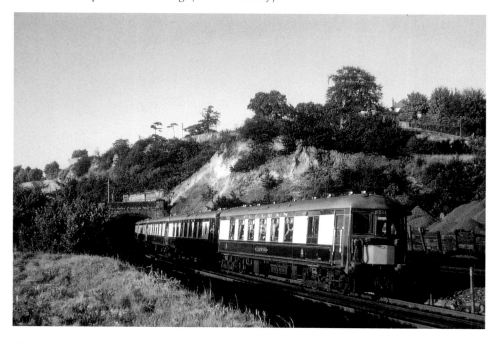

The Belle emerges from Redhill (Sand) Tunnel on 24 July 1967. Earlswood Goods Depot is on the right, Redhill MPD to the left. (*John Scrace*)

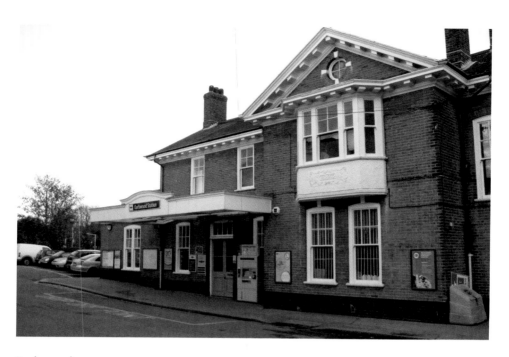

Earlswood

Earlswood station building proclaims its date of birth (AD 1905) beneath the first floor bay window. This dates from the quadrupling to Balcombe Tunnel Junction, but a station existed here from August 1868. (*Rod Lucas*)

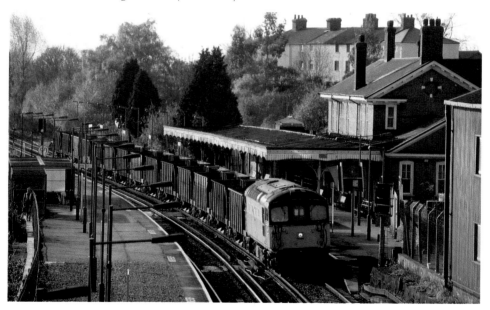

Class 33 diesel loco 33108 hauls the 7Y73 Three Bridges to Woking PW train through Earlswood in November 1992, showing the valanced canopy on the up platform and the rather primitive accommodation on the down platform. Both fast line platforms have now been taken out of use and partially removed. (*Alex Dasi-Sutton*)

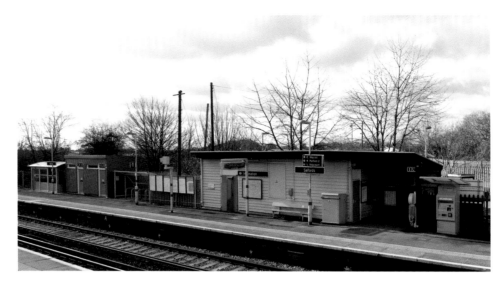

Salfords

Salfords halt was opened in October 1915 with a very limited service to serve local factories (principally the Monotype works). A full service was introduced once the line was electrified to Three Bridges in July 1932 and the station ceased to be a halt from January 1935. Recently, joint funding from Southern and Surrey County Council has paid for station improvements. Salfords' up platform now boasts (from left to right) an enclosed, heated waiting room with automatic door entry; male and female toilets (with disabled access and baby changing facilities); new signage; a ticket machine; departures information (including outside the station); and a refurbished footbridge. It is seen on 2 February 2013. (*Simon Jeffs*)

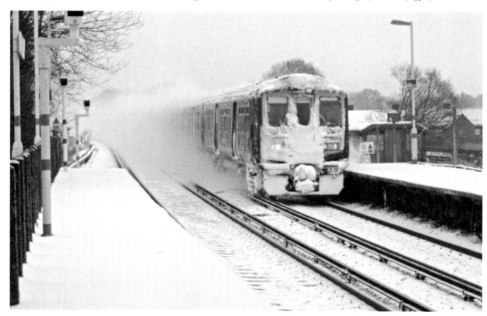

Salfords is a good location to watch the trains go by, but our photographer was certainly braving the elements to get this shot of 319446 on a very inclement 2 February 2009. (*Ian Buck*)

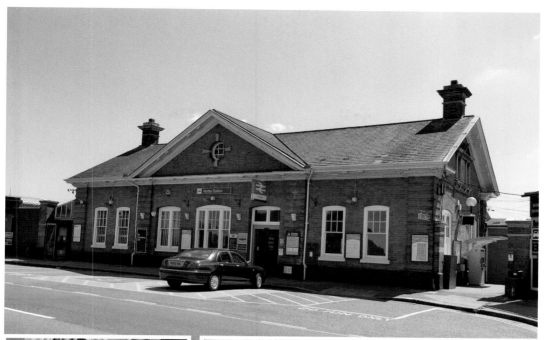

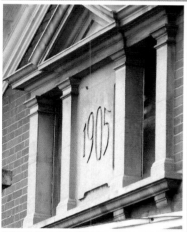
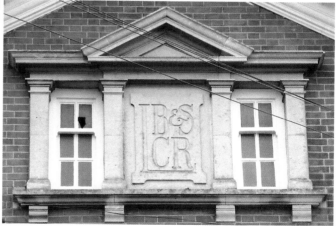

Horley

The current neo-Georgian station buildings, like Earlswood, date from the 1904/5 quadrupling. Date and ownership are displayed under both end wall gables (*inserts*). (*Laurel Arnison/David Gosling*)

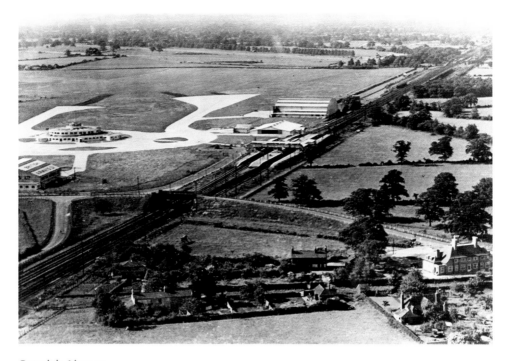

Gatwick Airport
A wonderful photo of the 'Beehive' air terminal and the station from around 1937. Note the sidings north of the station and the Greyhound public house in the foreground. (*Gatwick Airport Public Relations*)

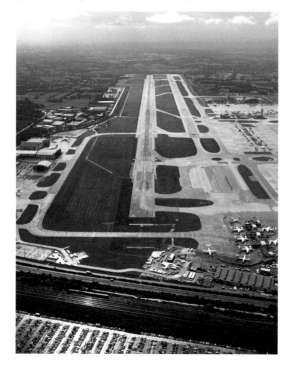

The contrast with this 2012 view could not be greater! The main (*left*) and emergency (*right*) runways are seen. The South and North terminals are off-picture to the right. A Class 166 DMU waits in the sidings to return to Reading.
(*Gatwick Airport Public Relations*)

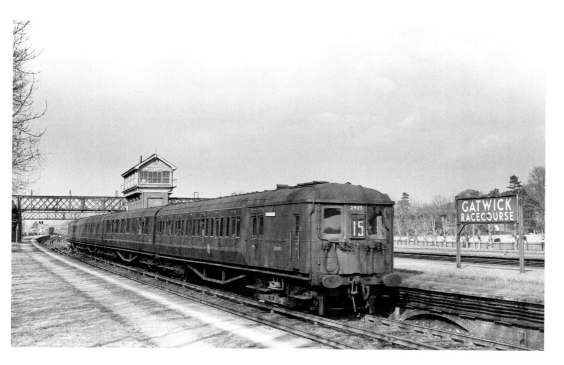

The 'New' Gatwick Airport station was the former Gatwick Racecourse station, where 4 Lav unit 2925 calls on 17 March 1956. (*J. J. Smith*)

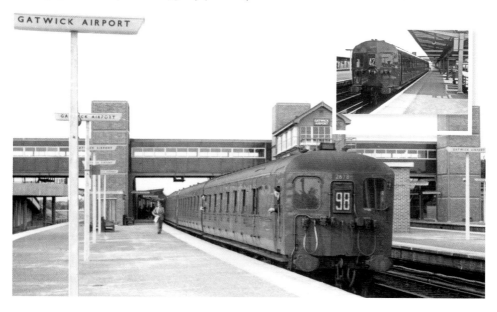

Open for the Airport. 2 Hal 2678 calls with a Bognor Regis train on 30 August 1958. (*J. H. Aston*)
Inset: The first 'Gatwick Express': After the new airport station opened in 1958, an EMU such as 'Tin' 2 Hal 2699, above, was attached/detached to a Bognor Regis–Victoria semi-fast service. (*Ray Glover*)

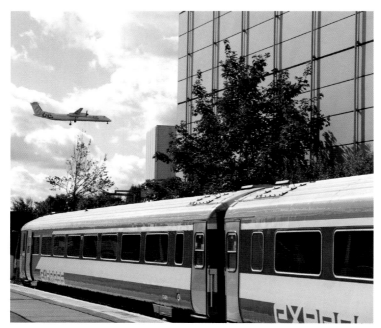

Gatwick Express now: Gatwick Express services are now operated by the 1988-vintage Class 442 units. Although giving a quiet and smooth ride, the lack of wide, sliding doors and reduced luggage space compared to the 460s is a retrograde step. A flybe Bombardier Q400 passes over on 19 September 2012. (*Simon Jeffs*)

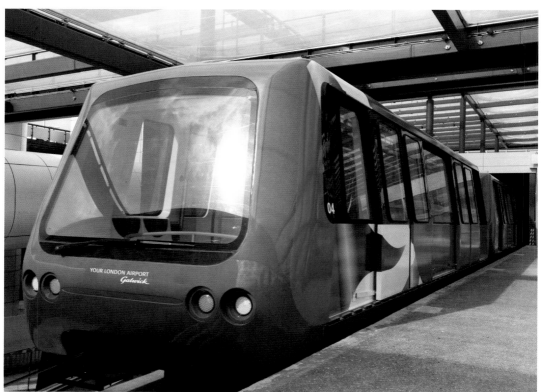

There is another railway (technically, a monorail) at Gatwick Airport, the shuttle connecting the South and North Terminals. (*Gatwick Airport Public Relations*)

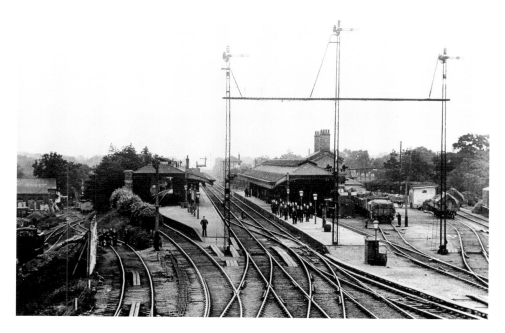

Three Bridges

Originally a tiny hamlet, Three Bridges station opened with the coming of the London & Brighton Railway in July 1841. The importance of Three Bridges increased with the opening of the lines to Horsham in 1848 and East Grinstead in 1855, when the station was enlarged. Platforms 4–6 (*above*) date from this period. The view shows the station before the 1907 quadrupling, with the first engine shed on the extreme left. (*Lens of Sutton*)

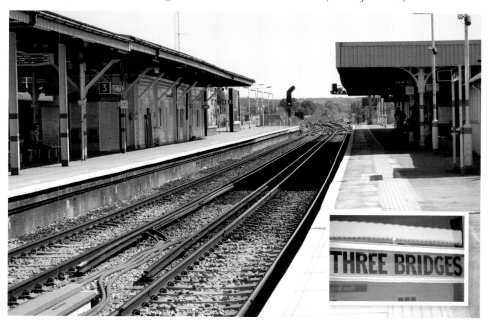

1907 buildings remain on platforms 1/2 and 3/4. The waiting room on Platform 1/2 includes this etched signage (*insert*). (*Laurel Arnison*)

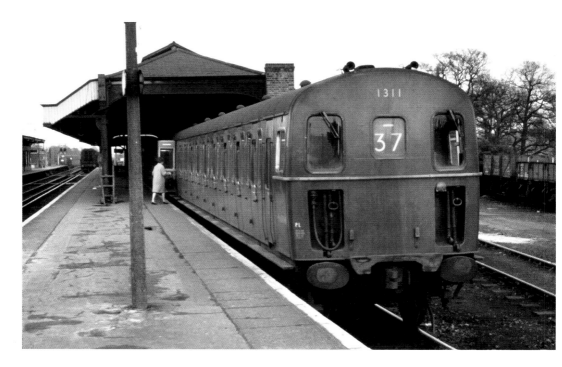

Platform 6 served the East Grinstead branch. The canopy dates from before the quadrupling but was removed in May 1965. A 3D DEMU waits to depart in 1960. The 1983 Signalling Centre now occupies the area. (*Colour-Rail*)

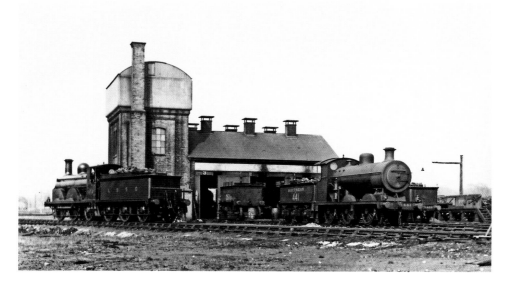

A new motive power depot (MPD) was established in the fork between the Brighton and Horsham lines in 1911 and remained open until June 1964, although it continued to stable diesel and electro-diesel locos until demolition in the mid-1970s. A transitional view on 1 May 1926 sees Gladstone 0-4-2 B172 *Littlehampton*, still in LBSCR livery, and a C2X 0-6-0 No. 441 in Southern branding. (*H. C. Casserley*)

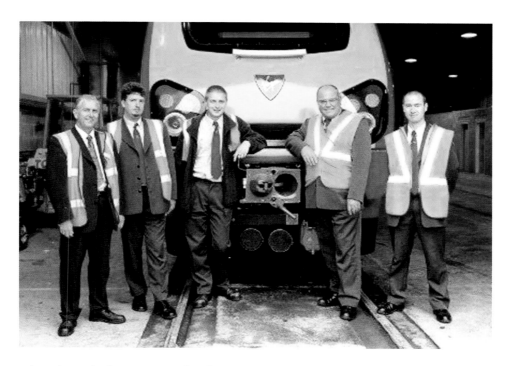

A brand new facility to service the Class 220 Voyager DMUs introduced onto CrossCountry services between Brighton and the North was opened on the site of the old MPD in 2001. This had a very short life, being mothballed with the withdrawal of CrossCountry services to Sussex in 2008. It was demolished in the spring of 2012. However, Three Bridges is set for a renaissance as one of two service depots for the new Greater Thameslink franchise's rolling stock. Work commenced on this enormous facility, which will take over the entire former up and downside yards and the site of the MPD, in spring 2012. (*Paul Edwards*)

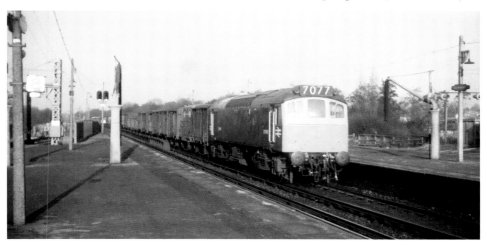

Under the Southern Railway, the upside yard became a major PW depot for the Civil Engineers and despatched ballast and works trains all over the Southern system until closure in around 2005. A Class 25 loco D7655 passes with a goods train for Brighton in March 1968. (*Gordon Gravett*)

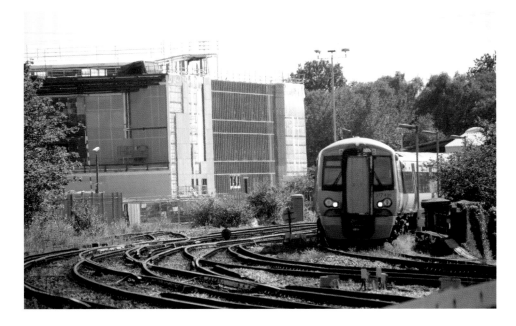

The Signalling Centre will be superseded by one of Network Rail's Integrated Electronic Control Centres, which will take over the areas now controlled by Victoria, London Bridge and West Hampstead SCCs from 2014. It will also house the Control Centre currently located at East Croydon. Construction of this new facility, which is located to the east of the former Voyager depot, was well-advanced in July 2012. (*Laurel Arnison*)

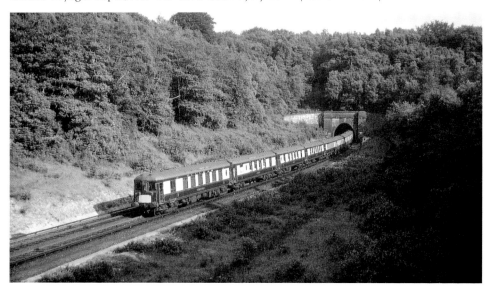

Balcombe Tunnel
The north portal of Balcombe Tunnel is seen on 15 June 1968 with the Belle emerging. The River Mole runs through the sandstone ridge above the tunnel bore, which is lined with lead to minimise the drips of water that percolate through! The countryside hereabouts is very attractive. (*John Scrace*)

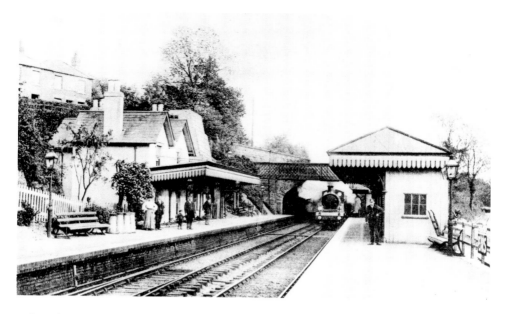

Balcombe

The station remains delightfully rural and only sees one up or down service an hour off peak. This Edwardian view depicts a London train approaching under the narrow bridge abutting onto the sandstone rocks that abut the down side of the station. (*John Minnis Collection*)

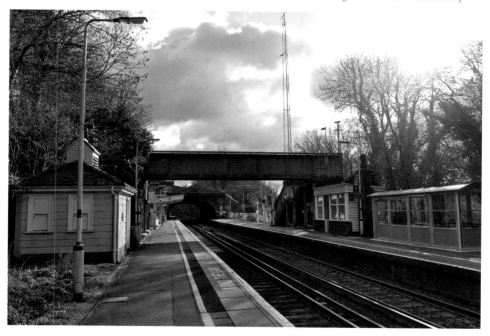

The snowdrops were out in this view taken on 2 February 2013. The footbridge has moved further down the platform, the upside waiting rooms have been replaced, the platforms have been extended and only the lower storey of the downside station house remains. (*Simon Jeffs*)

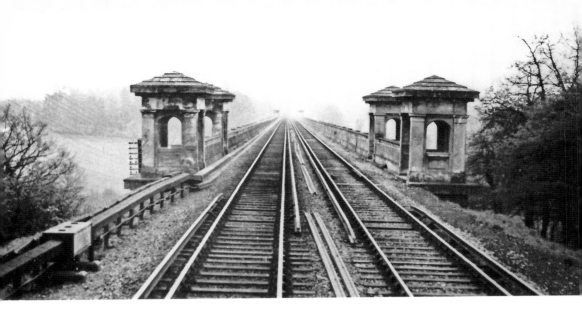

Ouse Valley Viaduct

Described as 'one of the most magnificent undertakings ever constructed', the viaduct is 462 yards long, with thirty-seven arches up to 100 feet high with classical 'Villas' at each end. There are superb views to the Nymans estate to the west and Ardingly College to the east. It is amazing to think that the millions of bricks to build the viaduct were conveyed by barge along the tiny River Ouse far below. The driver's view is seen above in 1937 (*H. C. Casserley*), while the view from the ground (*below*) allows one to appreciate the viaduct's graceful proportions. A Class 73 electro-diesel locos heads a van train at sunset on 17 September 1966. (*Gordon Gravett*)

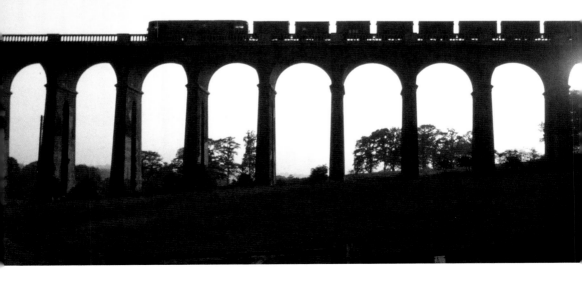

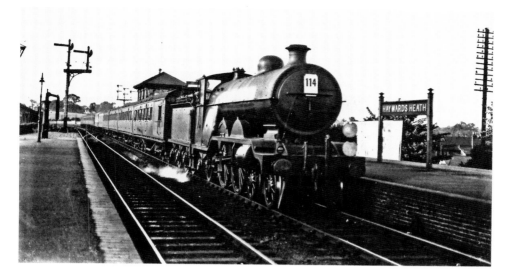

Haywards Heath

One of the beautiful Marsh Class H2 4-4-2 Atlantics, No. B421, *South Foreland*, arrives on a summer evening, 19 July 1930, with the 5.40 p.m. Victoria–West Worthing service. The station is still an LBSCR creation. However, in connection with the 1932 electrification, it was completely rebuilt into the latest Southern Railway style with two 800-foot island platforms and is the best example of its kind on the line. (*H. C. Casserley*)

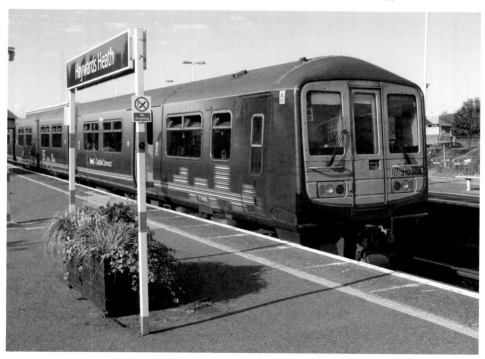

A view north sees one of the colourful First Capital Connect Class 319 units on a Bedford service on the evening of 22 July 2012. (*Simon Jeffs*)

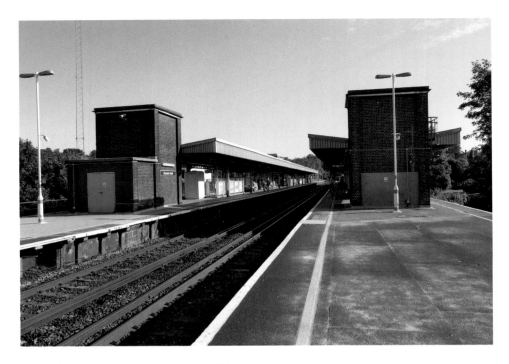

Meanwhile, the view south shows the lift towers and long canopies on the island platforms. The architecture is functional rather than arresting. (*Laurel Arnison*)

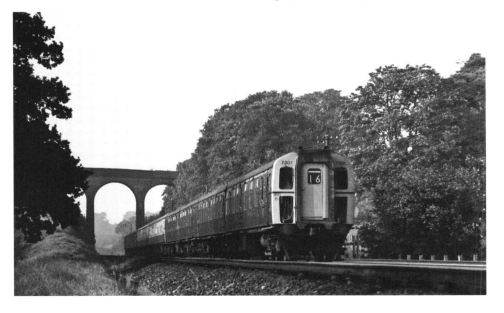

Wivelsfield
Between Haywards Heath and Wivelsfield, the line passes through a deep cutting crossed by this graceful three-arched bridge. A Cig/Big/Cig formation heads for Eastbourne in this 1968 view. Folly Hill Tunnel, with Haywards Heath station beyond, can be glimpsed in the distance. (*Michael Baker*)

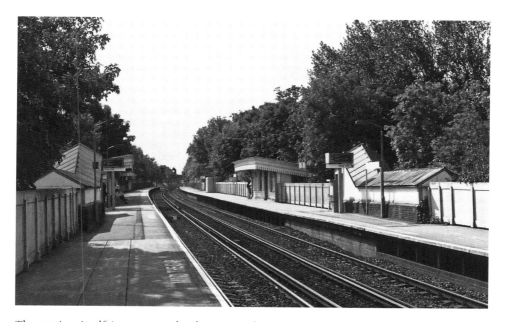

The station itself is on an embankment, with separate entrances to each platform from the road underbridge at the London end of the station. Platforms and fences are the products of the Southern Railway's Exmouth Junction concrete factory in this view from 17 September 1991. The down side one is still the LBSCR structure. Keymer Junction, where the Eastbourne line bears left, is just beyond the distant overbridge. (*John Scrace*)

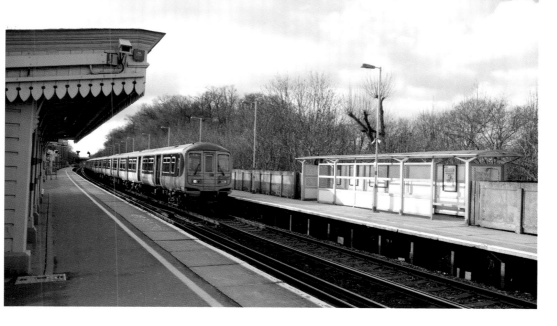

By 2013, the upside waiting room is an open steel and glass structure (there is a second one obscured by the approaching Class 319 unit), while the LBSCR downside structure has been opened out. Both entrances to the subway remain. (*Simon Jeffs*)

83

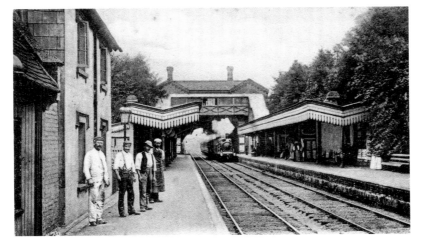

Burgess Hill
A wonderful period postcard from the end of the nineteenth century shows the station staff and a Brighton train approaching. (*John Minnis Collection*)

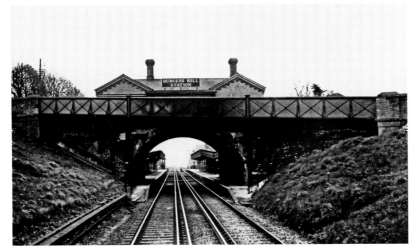

A driver's view shows the station buildings and the canopies over the platforms in 1937. (*H. C. Casserley*)

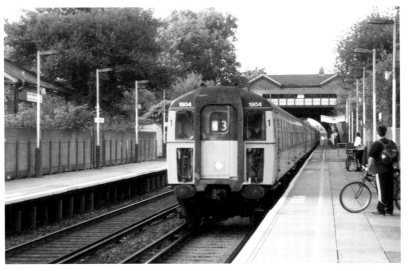

By 19 August 2003, little had changed. The station house has gone, but the canopies, station buildings on the overbridge and goods shed (albeit disused) are still intact. A Connex-liveried Class 421 arrives with a London Bridge to Littlehampton via Hove working. (*Tony Rispoli*)

84

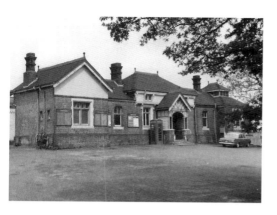 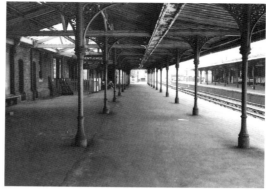

Hassocks

This station now bears no resemblance to these two views taken on 21 May 1972. Both the neat up side station building, which resembles that preserved on the Bluebell Railway at Sheffield Park, and the wide canopies with the ornate ironwork on the stanchions were all swept away in the 1970s (admittedly, they were in a dangerous condition), to be replaced by a very uninspiring set of glass and steel structures. (*John Scrace*)

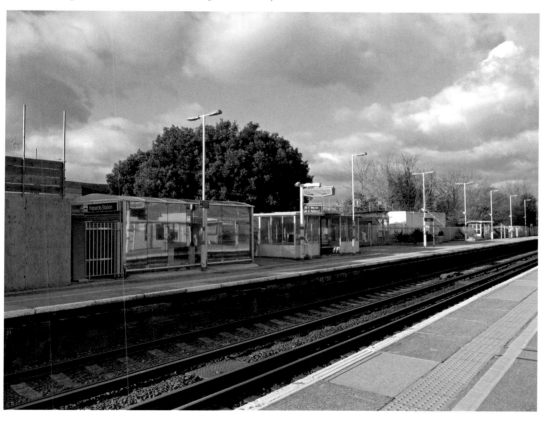

Building work, to a design agreed with local residents, had commenced on the new upside station buildings in January 2013. Currently, (February 2013) the booking office and toilets are in portakabins but steel and glass waiting rooms are still intact. (*Simon Jeffs*)

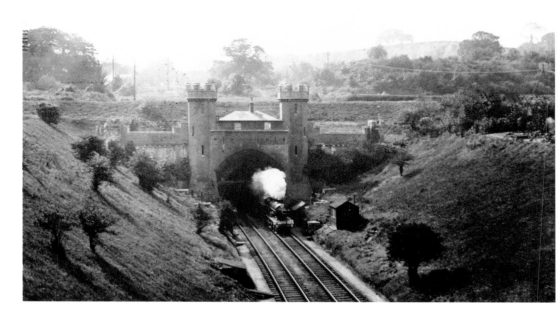

Clayton Tunnel

An up express, headed by a B4 4-4-0 loco, emerges from the tunnel in this Edwardian-era photo. (*John Minnis Collection*)

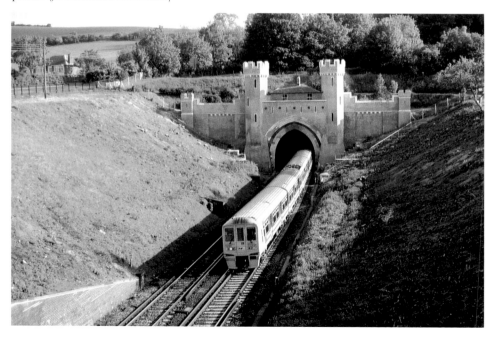

In the EMU era, Class 319 unit 319 185 emerges from the newly cleaned and renovated north portal of Clayton tunnel on 1 June 1996 with the 16:57 Brighton–Bedford service. Clayton Tunnel is notorious for the terrible accident between three trains on 25 August 1861 in which twenty-three people died. (*Colin Scott-Morton*)

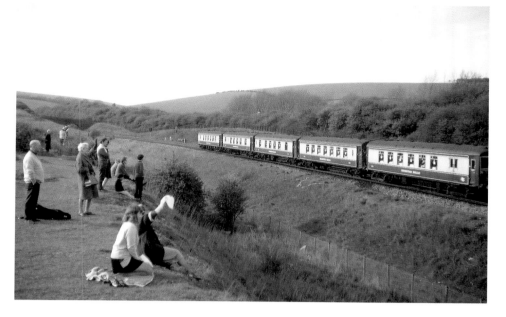

Patcham

Goodbye to the Belle! 5 Bel unit 3051 heads past the crowds at Patcham on a special during the final day of service, Sunday 30 April 1972. The green fields between Clayton and Patcham tunnels have mostly been lost to road developments, and this view could not be photographed so easily now. (*John Scrace*)

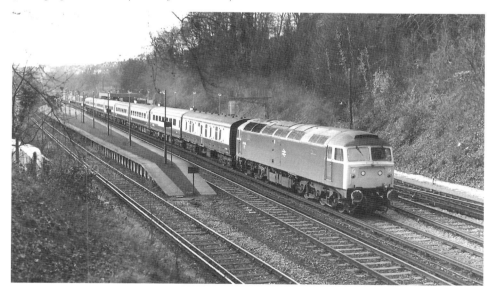

Preston Park

Nearly at Brighton, Preston Park station in the north Brighton suburbs sees heavy commuter traffic. Four tracks were available on 5 April 1983, but the down loop was lifted soon after. The 09:20 Brighton–Manchester Piccadilly service, headed by 47486, heads north. (*John Scrace*)

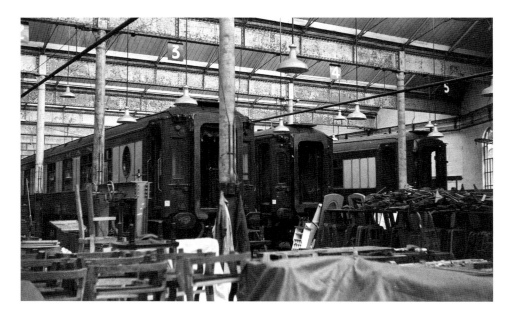

Journey's End – Brighton

As we enter the Brighton station area, on our right is the site of the former Pullman Car Company's workshops, where craftsmen would overhaul or even rebuild Pullman cars from all parts of the UK, including those from the 5 Bel units, between 1928 and 1963. There were plans to use the site as a transport museum and several items, including two ex-Bel cars (Nos. 292 and 293), were stored here until the project was abandoned in 2008. The works have now been demolished. (*J. J. Smith*)

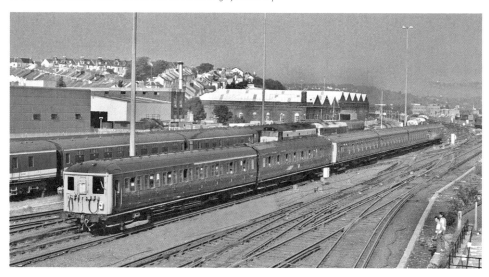

Next on the right is Brighton Traction and Rolling Stock Maintenance Depot, otherwise known as Lover's Walk. During the Brighton Open Day on 21 September 1991, held to celebrate the 150th anniversary of the opening of the line to Brighton, preserved 2Bil No. 2090 and 4Sub No. 4732 worked a shuttle service to and from Seaford. Lover's Walk is on the right, with an array of steam, diesel and electric locos, plus EMUs, for enthusiasts to enjoy. (*Brian Morrison*)

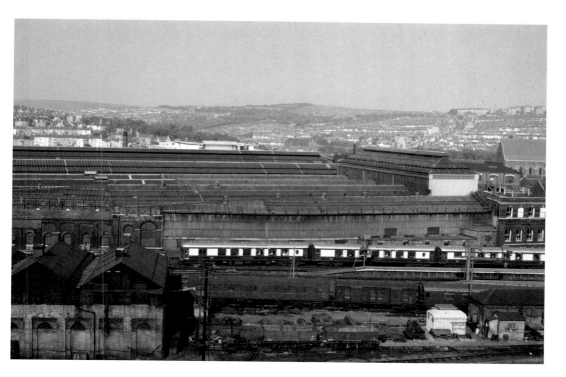

This view across the station, taken in the early 1960s, shows the extent of the locomotive works in the background and part of the steam shed in the foreground. (*Colour-Rail*)

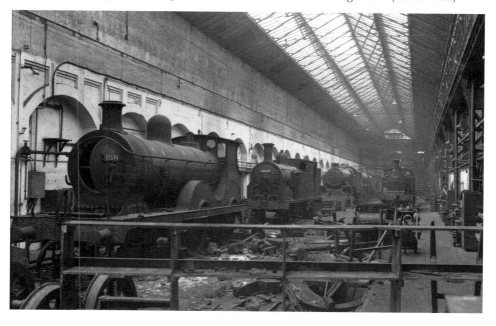

The Works Repair Shop in 1952 hosts a variety of steam locos. In the left-hand row are D Class 4-4-0 31574, M7 Class 0-4-4T 30039 and two Fairburn 2-6-4T engines, with 42074 at the front. On the right, another M7, 30372. (*Brian Jackson Collection*)

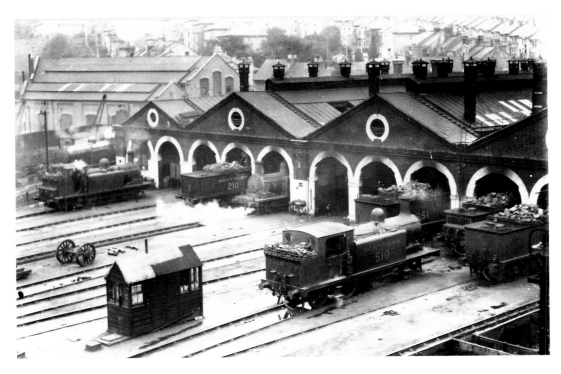

Two views of Brighton Shed. First, from 1927, with E4 0-6-2T Radial tank 510 prominent. This loco was later transferred to work in the Isle of Wight. (*H. C. Casserley*)

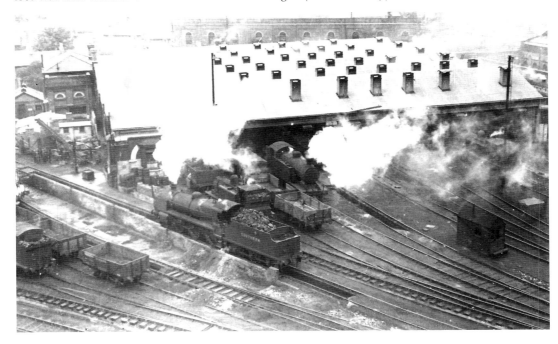

Next, we move on to 1946. The shed has been rebuilt and a Maunsell 2-6-0 locomotive awaits its next job. (*H. C. Casserley*)

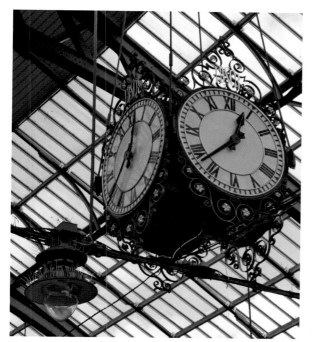
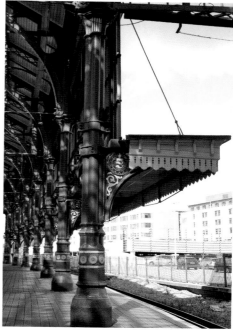

The LBSCR clock, recently restored, still stands over the concourse (*left*). While platforms 9 and 10 have been removed, a valanced canopy supported by ornate columns still shelters passengers on Platform 8 (*middle*), and the spandrels contain the Brighton coat of arms (*right*). (*Simon Jeffs*)

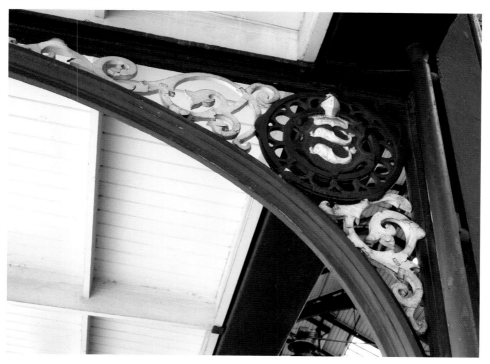

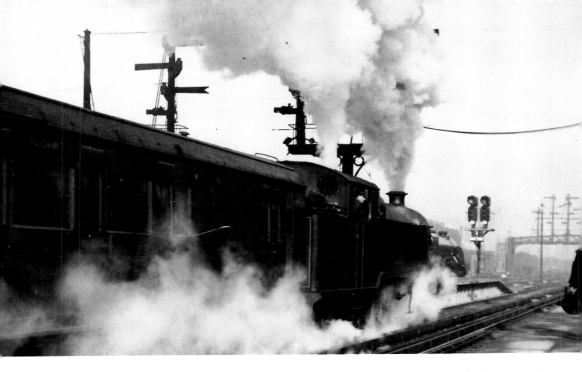

The 09:20 city express to London Bridge waits to leave Brighton in October 1932, the last year of express steam. L Class 4-6-4T No. 332 *Stroudley* is in charge (*H. C. Casserley*)

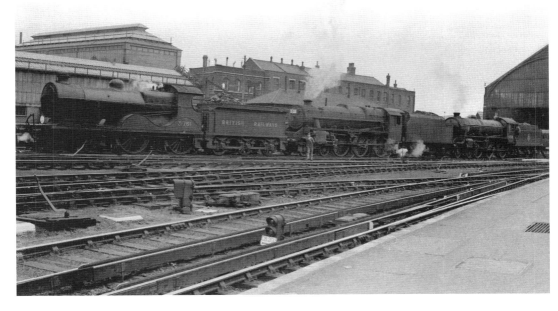

Just about anything could turn up at Brighton on a Bank Holiday excursion. This remarkable line-up (from left to right) shows locos after servicing at Brighton shed on 21 June 1952: L Class 31761, LMS Black 5 45071 and B1 class 61138. The Eastern Region B1 was believed to be one of the first to visit Brighton and had arrived with an excursion from Cambridge. (*Brian Jackson*)

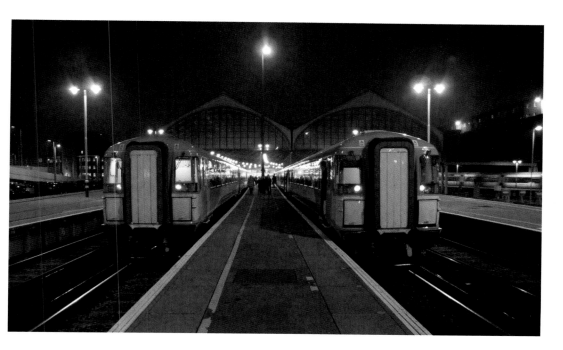

The latest trains at Brighton are the Class 442 units. These are used on Southern's hourly semi-fast services to Victoria and on peak period Gatwick Expresses to provide extra capacity to accommodate Brighton's enormous commuter traffic. (*Colin Scott-Morton*)

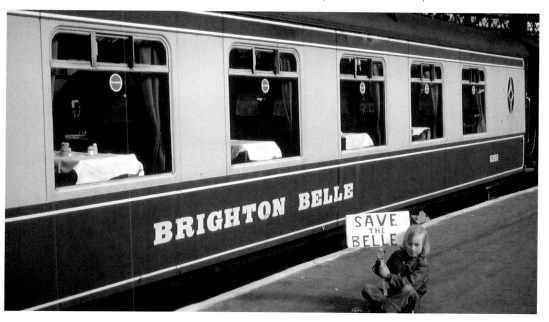

Let us finish our journey with the most glamorous Brighton train of all – the Brighton Belle. This young protestor making his feelings felt on the last day of service will be glad to know that the Belle will live again! The 5 Bel Trust is bringing back the Brighton Belle and is currently restoring six cars at its base in Barrow Hill, Derbyshire. (*Clinton Shaw*)

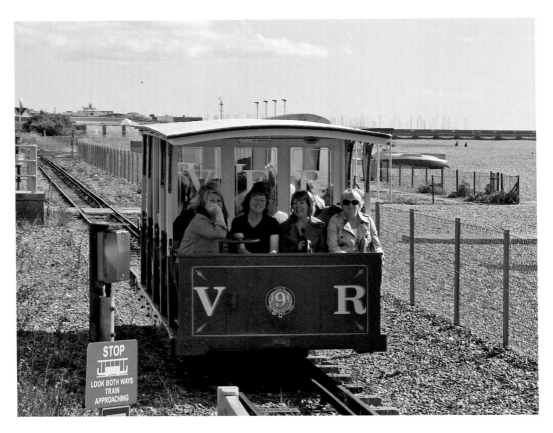

After your trip to Brighton, I'm sure you will wish to visit the seafront. So, don't forget to visit Volk's Electric Railway, running from the Palace Pier to Black Rock near the Marina. This was Britain's first public electric railway, opened in 1883 and still going strong today. Four 'Brighton Belles' enjoy their trip on 29 September 2012. (*Simon Jeffs*)

Bibliography

Anon. 1972. *1948 British Railway Locomotives* (reprint). Ian Allan.

Baker, M. H. C. 1989. *London to Brighton. 150 Years of Britain's Premier Holiday Line.* Patrick Stephens Ltd.

Bayliss, D. A. 1981. *Retracing the First Public Railway.* Living History Publications (Croydon).

Brown, D. 2008. *Southern Electric: A New History. Volume 1 – Development of the London Suburban Network and its Trains.* Capital Transport Publishing.

Brown, D. 2010. *Southern Electric: A New History. Volume 2 – Main Line Electrification, the War Years and British Railways.* Capital Transport Publishing.

Bonavia, M. R. 1987. *The History of the Southern Railway.* Unwin Hyman.

Conolly, W. P. 1988. *British Railways Pre-Grouping Atlas and Gazetteer* (4th Edn). Ian Allan.

Cooper, B. K. 1981. *Rail Centres: Brighton.* Ian Allan.

Faulkner, J. N. 1991. *Rail Centres: Clapham Junction.* Ian Allan.

Grant, S. 2011. *The LBSCR Elevated Electrification: A Pictorial View of Construction.* Noodle Books.

Grant, S. & Jeffs, S. 2012. *The Brighton Belle – The Story of a Famous and Much-Loved Train.* Capital Transport Publishing.

Gray, A. *The London to Brighton Line 1841–1977.* The Oakwood Press.

Hamilton Ellis, C. 1960. *The London Brighton and South Coast Railway.* Ian Allan.

Jackson, A. A. 1985. *London's Termini* (2nd Edn.). David & Charles.

Jacobs, G. (Editor). 2008. *Railway Track Diagrams Book 5: Southern and TfL* (3rd Edn). TRACKmaps.

Marsden, C. J. 1983. *Southern Electric Multiple Units, 1898-1948*

Marsden, C. J. 1983. *Southern Electric Multiple Units, 1948-1983*

Minnis, J. 1999. *Images of Railways. The London, Brighton & South Coast Railway.* Tempus Publishing Ltd.

Mitchell V. & Smith K. 1986. *Three Bridges to Brighton.* Middleton Press.

Mitchell V. & Smith K. 1987. *Victoria to East Croydon.* Middleton Press.

Mitchell V. & Smith K. 1988. *London Bridge to East Croydon.* Middleton Press.

Mitchell V. & Smith K. 1988. *East Croydon to Three Bridges.* Middleton Press.

Moody, G. T. 1979. *Southern Electric 1909–1979* (5th Edn.). Ian Allan.

Morris, O. J. 19xx. *Railways Before the Grouping, Number One – L.B.& S.C.R.* Ian Allan.

Nock, O. S. 1966. *Southern Steam.* Pan Books Ltd. (1972 paperback reprint)

Pallant, N. & Bird, D. 1984. *BR Locomotives: 1. Diesel and Electric Locomotives of the Southern Region.* Ian Allan

Pretious, P. 2009. *Southern Railway Locomotive Headcodes.* MHRPS – Alton Information Office Publication.

Rayner, B. 1975. *Southern Electrics: A Pictorial Survey.* D. Bradford Barton Ltd.

Skinner, M. W. G. 1985. *Croydon's Railways.* Kingfisher Railway Productions.

Southern Electric Group. 1984. *Southern Region Two Character Headcodes* (7th Edn). Southern Electric Group.

Tayler, A. 2004. *A Lifetime in Traction. An Engineer on the Southern Diesels and Electrics.* KRB Publications.

Walmsley, T. 2008. *Shed by Shed Part 5: Steam Locomotives Allocated to Sheds 70A to 75G 1950–1968.* St Petroc InfoPublishing.

Welch, M. 2004. *Southern DEMUs.* Capital Transport Publishing.

White, H. P. 1969. *A Regional History of the Railways of Great Britain: Volume 2 – Southern England* (3rd Edn). David & Charles.

White, H. P. 1971. *A Regional History of the Railways of Great Britain: Volume 3 – Greater London* (2nd Edn). David & Charles.

White, H. P. 1976. *Forgotten Railways: South-East England.* David & Charles.

Acknowledgements

First and foremost, I must thank my wife, Laurel, who not only accompanies me on photography outings but has nursed me through over thirty years of 'Railway Enthusiasts' Disease'! Second, I must thank the numerous photographers who have provided images from their collections to use in this book, in particular – John Scrace, Chris Wilson, Brian Morrison, Alex Dasi-Sutton, Don Benn, John Atkinson, David Brown, Tony Rispoli, Brian Jackson, Bryan Rayner, Lester Hayes, Michael Baker, Peter Jones, Colin Scott-Morton, Gordon Gravett, J. H. Aston and Paul Edwards. Richard Casserley very kindly lent me many photos taken by his father, H. C. Casserley; Tony Hillman provided photos from the J. J. Smith collection, kept at the Bluebell Railway Museum; John Minnis sourced wonderful images from the LBSCR era; John Wills' website, www.southernrailway.net, provided many rare images as did Paul Edwards' monumental site on the Brighton motive power depots, http://thebrightonmotivepowerdepots.yolasite.com/brighton-loco.php. From the professional railway, Chris Pancutt, Southern Corporate Relations, arranged authority for Laurel and myself to take photos at many stations along the line, whose staff were unfailingly polite and helpful. Gatwick Airport Public Relations provided some stunning images of the airport and Network Rail assisted with photos of the Thameslink Project. Laurie Mack, John Minnis and Tony Hillman proof-read the text, so any errors remaining are my own. Finally, I'd like to thank my father, Stanley Jeffs, who introduced me to the Brighton line, running past the bottom of the pub garden of The Greyhound, Tinsley Green, thus giving me a life-long love of the Southern Electric.

Simon Jeffs
Eastbourne